RUPERT CHAW
Rugby in 1887, w
school. After bein
won a scholarship
Cambridge, where
became the centre
world, and his first
1909. A collection
1911 and in 1912 Brooke won a fellowship to
King's, but, following a serious breakdown, he
spent the next year travelling in the US,
Canada, and the Pacific, where he wrote further
poems. On the outbreak of the First World War
he joined the RNVR. In 1915 his five famous
'War Sonnets' appeared in *New Numbers*, and
Brooke was hailed as the leading poet of his
generation. However, Brooke was already en
route to the Dardanelles where he died of
blood-poisoning and was buried on the Isle of
Scyros. The news of his death was received with
great sadness in Britain but Brooke's reputation
as a poet grew after his death with the
posthumous publication of *1914 and Other
Poems* in 1915.

TIMOTHY ROGERS read English at Brooke's
old college, King's, before embarking on a
distinguished teaching career, which saw him,
before his recent retirement, as first Principal of
the Bosworth College, Leicestershire. He met
many of Brooke's friends and relatives during
research for his previous highly acclaimed study
Rupert Brooke: A Reappraisal and Selection
(Routledge and Kegan Paul, 1971). He has also
edited *Georgian Poetry 1911–12* in the Critical
Heritage series, and a collection of children's
verse entitled *Those First Affections*. Mr Rogers
now lives in Cambridge, where he is currently
editing the Norwegian and Icelandic journals of
the painter Keith Grant.

the Poems of Rupert Brooke

A Centenary Edition

including hitherto unpublished poems
Edited and introduced by Timothy Rogers

BLACK SWAN

THE POEMS OF RUPERT BROOKE
A Centenary Edition

A BLACK SWAN BOOK   0 552 99284 4

First publication in Great Britain

PRINTING HISTORY
Black Swan edition published 1987

Introduction copyright © Timothy Rogers 1987

This book is set in 10/11 pt Garamond
by Colset Private Limited, Singapore.

Black Swan Books are published by Transworld
Publishers Ltd., 61–63 Uxbridge Road, Ealing,
London W5 5SA, in Australia by Transworld
Publishers (Australia) Pty. Ltd., 15–23 Helles
Avenue, Moorebank, NSW 2170, and in
New Zealand by Transworld Publishers (N.Z.)
Ltd., Cnr. Moselle and Waipareira Avenues,
Henderson, Auckland.

Made and printed in Great Britain by
The Guernsey Press Co. Ltd., Guernsey, Channel Islands.

Acknowledgments

Three debts I owe to Rupert Brooke. First for his own writing, both in verse and prose, some of which I have come to value more highly as the years have passed, though much of it less so than on my youthful first acquaintance. Which is partly accounted for by my second debt, for Brooke's poems took me in those early years to Swinburne, even to Dowson, among those poets he admired in youth, and later and more rewardingly to Donne, Webster, and other Elizabethans.

My third debt to Brooke is for the interestingness and generosity of his friends, almost all of whom – apart from those whose lives, like his, were cut short by the First World War – achieved distinction in their various fields. More than forty years have passed since I first, as a schoolboy, wrote to Lady Violet Bonham Carter about him, and she, in the course of a helpful correspondence, asked if I were writing a life. From that moment I *was*. And, though I never thought that my early attempt was worth publishing, a judgment which was amply confirmed by Christopher Hassall's monumental work, I acquired valuable material from surviving friends, of whom many had, alas, died when Hassall came to write.

I was able to draw upon this material when, in 1971, I published what I then naïvely supposed might be the final product of the Brooke industry which was threatening to overwhelm its fascinating but minor subject. *Rupert Brooke: a Reappraisal and Selection* aimed to provide all that was necessary by way of reappraisal, both biographical and critical, together with the best of his verse and prose. On the principle that Brooke had written no more, and arguably fewer, than a dozen really fine poems, and that, if he had lived, he would almost certainly have excluded the superabundance of what he himself called 'unimportant prettiness', I was stringent in my selection, including for example only two of the '1914' sonnets (though even they would not be in my dozen). But the book went quickly out of print – it is now a rarity – while both the Marsh and Keynes editions of the poems continued to sell in their tens of thousands.

Moreover, two further full-length studies of Brooke have since appeared, and I have to allow that the second, John Lehmann's *Rupert Brooke: his Life and his Legend*, provides what is in many ways the most balanced account to date. I have been happy to draw on it, particularly in relation to Brooke's sexual life, in further balancing my introduction.

I am grateful to Dr Jon Stallworthy and Brooke's present trustees for confirming and extending the permission granted me by the late Sir Geoffrey Keynes, friend, editor, bibliographer and formerly senior trustee, to include hitherto unpublished and copyright material. I must also thank my first publishers, Routledge and Kegan Paul, for allowing me to draw on my earlier book, as also upon my *Georgian Poetry 1912–1922* in their 'Critical Heritage' series. Going further back, I am grateful now, as before, to a former editor of *The Times Literary Supplement* for permission to draw upon my reviews of Hassall's biography and of the Penguin *Georgian Poetry* (28 May 1964 and 23 February 1962 respectively), and to a former editor of *English* for permission to draw from an article (Autumn 1968) which led directly to the recrudescence of my early study.

I must express my thanks to a former Librarian of King's College, Cambridge, the late Dr A. N. L. Munby, for invaluable help in the past; to the present Modern Literary Archivist, Dr Michael Halls, for invaluable help in the present; and to the Provost and Fellows of Brooke's and my College for their continuing hospitality.

Finally it is to Brooke's friends that I must return. One of the fascinations of talking with them was to discover how each had known, and treasured as 'the real Rupert', a different person. Something of this chameleon quality is discernible in his letters: one remembers Keats on the 'Camelion Poet' who has no identity, but 'lives in gusto' – I wish I had the art to convey Brooke's multifariousness. Sir Edward Marsh, Dr Hugh (later Lord) Dalton, Walter de la Mare, Gwen Raverat, Professors Edward J. Dent, J. B. Trend and Albert Rutherstan, Sir John Sheppard, Arthur Waley, John Masefield, Wilfred Gibson, Dudley Ward, Professor M. A. Lewis, Duncan Grant, have all contributed directly to my knowledge. As most were contemporaries of Brooke or older, and few people live to be a hundred, it is not surprising that they are all now dead. So, too, are the three friends to whom I owe most: Sir Geoffrey Keynes (though I often found myself differing with his judgments, I respected his devotion to Brooke and admired his persistence from his schooldays till his ninety-sixth year in collecting and preserving his manuscripts); Frances Cornford, from whom I learnt most about what matters most, Brooke's poetry; and Cathleen Nesbitt, who told me that I had 'got nearer to his personality than any one [she had] read'. To her and to Frances Cornford above all his friends must belong the chief credit for that.

Timothy Rogers,
Cambridge.:
5 November 1986.

Contents

Introduction

1 THE BROOKE MYTH

'Poets', writes Patrick Leigh-Fermor in *Roumeli*, 'have strange posthumous careers.' He recounts there the experience of a friend, Tanty Rodocanaki, on the Greek island of Skyros which Rupert Brooke had visited three days before his death and where, in a secluded olive grove, he lies buried. While Rodocanaki was reading the inscription on his grave, an old shepherd approached him.

> 'I see you are admiring the grave of *O Broukis*. He was a great poet. We are glad to have him with us. He was a good man.'

Intrigued by the conviction with which he spoke, Rodocanaki asked him what he thought of Brooke's poetry.

> 'I've never read any of it, I'm sorry to say,' the shepherd answered. 'I'm not strong on letters and foreign languages. But you could tell he was a great man. You see that old olive over there? That was his tree.'
> 'How do you mean?'
> 'He used to sit under it every day and write poetry.'

Rodocanaki asked if he was sure they were talking about the same person.

> 'Of course I am! *O Broukis* used to wander about the woods in silence, the very picture of an old-fashioned English gentleman.'
> 'What did he look like?'
> 'Magnificent, sir,' the shepherd answered. 'Tall, dignified, flowing hair, burning eyes and a long white beard.'

In considering for the year of his centenary the 'posthumous career' of Rupert Brooke, there may be some appropriateness in the image of a bearded wraith, *O Broukis*, remembered rather for his greatness than his poetry.

Because I take Rupert Brooke seriously as a poet, albeit a minor one (one hears his comment: 'One might as well speak of minor roses or minor sunsets!'), and because I know him to have been more widely gifted, more human, more cynical, more egotistical, and far far more interesting than the popular myth would have it, I shall seek to get the myth out of the way as far as is now possible: 'You cannot', he once said, 'smell flowers through a blanket.'

Perhaps the chief reason for adulation, both in his lifetime and after, was his remarkable looks. Nowadays one might hesitate to call a man beautiful: for his contemporaries there seemed to be no other word. John Galsworthy had 'rarely seen a man more beautiful'; Yeats called him 'the most beautiful young man in England'. The poet Frances Cornford, who came to know him as well as any of his friends, seemed to resent other people using the word to describe him, yet would do so herself, for 'it was an essential thing about him, how "lovely and pleasant" he was to look upon'. But she had seen him only a few times and had never spoken to him when she wrote the famous epigram which has always been published under its title, 'Youth'.

A young Apollo, golden-haired,
Stands dreaming on the verge of strife,
Magnificently unprepared
For the long littleness of life.

She always regretted that it should have been recognized as being about him, and privately recalled how, later, when she and Rupert were going through the proofs of her first book of poems early in 1910, they came to 'Youth'. She glanced sideways at him, hoping that he would not think it had anything to do with him (which by then it had not), but saw his shoulders stiffen, and a stern puritan profile of distaste, as he turned the page in silence.

How wrong was his biographer, Christopher Hassall, to claim that Rupert was unselfconscious! Of his first meeting with Henry James he remarked, 'I did the fresh boyish stunt, and it was a great success.' And when James said later, 'I do not see why he need be a poet', he was echoing (though possibly without knowing it) the *Punch* parody of Wilde: 'Why should he ever trouble to *be* anything? Why couldn't he be content to exist beautifully?' Rupert once asked his friend Gwen Raverat, 'Will you please disarrange my hair; I've got to read poetry to some old ladies.' And he himself suggested to Sherril Schell the neo-classical pose for that famous swan-neck photograph which his Cambridge friends used to call 'your favourite actress'. The Schellian (or

Shelleyan) Rupert is, indeed, part of the truth. But when one of his biographers, Maurice Browne, writes: 'When twenty-first century realists try to disentangle the man from the myth . . . they will be attempting a difficult task: the man *was* the myth', he is forgetting both the actor in him and the puritan.

Rupert Brooke has been poorly served by almost all his biographers. Sir Edward Marsh's *Memoir* was for long the chief source of biographical information. It was published with the *Collected Poems* in 1918, and Keynes records in his *Bibliography* that thirty-two impressions had been printed up to 1953, totalling 120,812 copies; thus for many readers it has provided the first and probably only introduction. Most of Rupert's friends hated the golden picture it gave and blamed Marsh for its selectivity. His mother complained to Frances Cornford that 'Eddie always seems to be thinking of Rupert's *fame*, and I can't stand it.' But it is clear now that she was no less responsible than he for the carefree laughing paragon who emerges in that she forbade all reference to 'romantic attachments, political socialism or private unhappiness'. The *Memoir* gave what was expected at the time: a memorial of a public reputation. The *Cambridge Review* declared: 'A legend has been endorsed. This life slips by like a panorama of earth's loveliest experiences.' Appropriately to his purpose, Marsh quotes 'Youth', adding that 'Mrs Cornford's epigram is well known, but one could not write about his great days at Cambridge without quoting it.'

One can understand the subsequent reticence of many of Brooke's friends, and several would-be biographers between the wars were deterred by their unwillingness to cooperate. Richard Halliburton, however, an American journalist and adventurer, managed to collect material from some of them – which is the more surprising when one gathers that it was his practice to dress up as 'Rupert Brooke' and announce himself as such on the doorstep. After Halliburton's death at sea in a Chinese junk, the material passed to a fellow countryman, Arthur Stringer, whose *Red Wine of Youth* (1948) was barred from publication in Great Britain 'until five years after the projected publication of the *Letters*' – for once one may applaud the guardianship of Keynes. Frances Cornford spoke of its 'complete crass *vulgarity*'. Poor Edward Marsh found himself counting references to 'the genial Eddie'. The figure who emerges from the text – 'the Apollonian youth', 'the wandering singer', 'the Cambridge Romeo', 'the poet of Grantchester', 'the son of Warwickshire', 'the carefree Epicurean', 'the brooding blue-domer', 'the island-hopper', 'the loquacious and long-haired King's student', 'the tawny-headed poet', 'the golden-haired officer' – is, surely, the *reductio ad absurdum* of the myth.

It is true that the Hassall biography (1964) and the *Letters* (1968) have done something to replace the myth with the man; but each of these official and monumental works suffers on the one hand from including too much that is trivial – 'boring' is a word which recurred in contemporary reviews – and on the other from an unfortunate censorship. Some of the difficulty, though not all, derives from Rupert's relationship with Ka Cox. It would be possible by putting Hassall's life and the *Letters* together to puzzle out something of its importance: it was, indeed, the major event of Brooke's life. But Geoffrey Keynes's selection from the letters (fewer than a quarter of those to Ka are included, and from these excisions are many and not always acknowledged) and his exclusion, for example, of those to James Strachey, make understanding difficult. Happily, as I have suggested, the short life by John Lehmann, which draws on both the Ka Cox and Strachey letters, provides a sensitive and much needed guide through this entanglement.

But why, it may be asked, is it necessary to concern oneself with Rupert Brooke's life, let alone the myth, when what matters, surely, is the poems? The answer must be two-fold. Many readers of poetry have been put off Brooke by a false picture of him, especially – as I shall recount in its place – by the 'canonization' which occurred when his early death *en route* for Gallipoli followed so closely on the fame of the '1914' sonnets. It is further true, and some might count this a weakness of the poems, that they are inseparably part of their author. Trelawny wrote of Shelley: 'To form a just idea of his poetry, you should have witnessed his daily life; his words and actions best illustrated his writings.' Edward Thomas wrote of Brooke: 'No one who knew him could easily separate him from his poetry: not that they were the same, but that the two inextricably mixed and helped one another.' Brooke's poems belong to the class of personal revelations: 'They share his secrets with the world', wrote Walter de la Mare, 'as if a boy had turned out the astonishing contents of his pockets just before going to bed.' They are all, apart from the obvious flights of fancy, true. Writing poetry was for him, not an act of dedication, but a means of self-expression, sometimes of self-discovery. His poems are a record of life as he reacted to it.

Perhaps I may add a tailpiece on the myth and its persistence. On a recent visit to Grantchester I lunched at what Rupert Brooke knew as the 'Rose and Crown'. An inn-sign which has since been replaced, worthy of *Red Wine of Youth* and recalling Brooke's comments on a photograph he was once sent in error for one of himself ('The soul of persons who write verse is said to be hermaphroditic, but not, I protest, *so* feminine'), proclaimed it as the 'Rupert Brooke'. In a place of honour within was a signed letter from Geoffrey Keynes bestowing on the renamed inn a limerick, 'unpublished', one would have hoped unpublishable. The menu – I swear it – offered 'Brookeburgers'.

2 THE LIFE

Rupert Chawner Brooke was born at Rugby on 3 August 1887. His father, William Parker Brooke, was a form master at Rugby School known to the boys as 'Tooler', who succeeded in 1902 to the housemastership of School Field. Rupert was to follow him in being both a classical scholar and a Fellow of King's College, Cambridge. His mother, Mary Ruth (*née*) Cotterill, was a remarkable woman, the dominant influence both in house and home. Rupert inherited something of her looks, especially the set of her eyes, her 'regard'. He also inherited something of her stubborn puritanism. When Lytton Strachey referred to him as 'Sarawak' (alluding to his namesake the famous Rajah), Rupert began referring to his mother as the Ranee. Throughout his life, though he chafed at her authority, he seemed never fully to escape from it.

He was the second of three brothers. Dick, who was six years older, died of pneumonia in January 1907. His death much affected Rupert, who was then in his first year at Cambridge; in 'The Call', the first of his poems to be published there, he imagines a reunion with him. With Alfred, who was three years younger and followed Rupert to King's, there was a still closer bond. He was killed two months after Rupert while serving as a lieutenant in the Post Office Rifles. One of his last injunctions to his mother had been that she should on no account believe the sentiments of the '1914' sonnets: war was horrible.

A second child, a girl, had died in infancy. Mrs Brooke, who was often shrewd in assessing character but pitifully ignorant of psychology, allowed Rupert to know how deeply she had hoped before his birth that she might have another daughter. He was to write later:

> I am here because at Fettes, in the seventies, Willie Brooke and Mary Cotterill got thrown together. And they had a son and a daughter, and the daughter died, and while the mother was thinking of the daughter another child was born, and it was a son, but in consequence of all this very female in parts – sehr dichterisch – me.

15

Hassall comments fairly that, although there was nothing effeminate about him, the fascination that there might be, and the fear that others might suppose there was, made him anxious to convince himself and them of his virility.

Rupert had a healthy dislike for his local preparatory school, Hillbrow, but he made some good friends there, notably James Strachey, the younger brother of Lytton, who was later to be analysed by Freud himself and to become his pupil and translator. A cousin of the Stracheys, Duncan Grant the future painter, was by three years their senior.

In 1906 Rupert entered Rugby School at the house which was already his home. This could have proved difficult for others, but, in the words of a schoolfriend, Hugh Russell Smith, though 'more than loyal to his father, . . . he never made it awkward for the rest of us. His sense of fun saw him through'. For himself, however, the close tie with home, especially with the Ranee, may have contributed to later difficulties and prolonged his adolescence. He was twenty-three when he wrote excitedly from Munich about a performance of Ibsen's *John Gabriel Borkman*: 'Therein is a youth who will fly from his mother in order to LIVE (it happens in Norway also).'

His school career was successful but not outstanding. He did the sort of things expected, then as now, of an English public schoolboy: he became head of his house, and played cricket and rugby football for the school. A report on him in *The Meteor*, the Rugby School magazine, as 'a reliable centre-three-quarter, who, though not brilliant, is usually in his place, and makes good openings', could be thought to have a wider, almost prophetic significance. But he also did things which were less expected, then as now, such as reading and writing poetry, and taking himself seriously as a follower of Swinburne.

He read a paper on Swinburne's *Atalanta in Calydon* to the sixth form discussion society, Eranos:

> The usual papers we have are on such subjects as *Hood* or *Calverley* – 'something to make you laugh'. . . . I saw my opportunity and took it. 'Have I not', I said, 'many a time and oft been bored beyond endurance by such Philistines? Now my revenge comes; I shall be merciless.' So I prepared a very long and profound paper full of beautiful quotations and read it to them for a very long time and they were greatly bored. They sat round in chairs and slumbered uneasily; while I in the centre ranted fragments of choruses, and hurled epithets upon them.

Rupert's thoughts on his paper were addressed to St John Lucas, a formative influence upon him in these early years. His family were neighbours of the Brookes, and he himself, at the time of Rupert's first letter to him in 1905, was a barrister in his mid-twenties. His first interest, however, was in poetry and contemporary – especially 'decadent' – literature. He was to edit the *Oxford Book of French Verse* (Rupert was to review it enthusiastically), and introduced his protégé to the poems of Baudelaire. The affectation of decadence which was to amuse Rupert for some years was certainly encouraged by Lucas, to whom he played up in conversation and in the mannered but self-mocking letters which survive.

Thus, in his last term at Rugby (May 1906), Rupert writes in a manner designed to please him:

> I am infinitely happy. I am writing nothing. I am content to live. After this term is over, the world awaits. But I do not now care what will come then. Only, my present happiness is so great that I fear the jealous gods will requite me afterwards with some terrible punishment, death perhaps – or life.

Thus, too, in his first month in Cambridge (October 1906) he writes to him:

> If only I were a poet I should love such a life very greatly, remembering moments of passion in tranquillity; but being first and chiefly only a boy I am restless and unable to read and write.

He concludes the letter:

> If you come to Cambridge at the end of the month you will see a performance of the Eumenides, in which an aged and grey-haired person called Rupert Brooke is wearily taking the part of the Herald. I put a long horn to my lips and pretend to blow and a villain in the orchestra simultaneously wantons on the cornet. It is very symbolical.

In another sense it was indeed symbolical. In his *Memoir* Edward Marsh, who had been in the first-night audience, remembered his first sight of Rupert as a 'radiant youthful figure in gold and vivid red and blue, like a Page in the Riccardi Chapel': an image which, says John Lehmann, 'has haunted the minds of many and stuck in the gullets of others'. Although he was never a good actor, a growing interest in drama was important both to himself and to history. A year after his début, he joined with his friend and namesake, Justin Brooke (then President of the Amateur Dramatic Club), to present Marlowe's *Dr Faustus*. It was to be the inaugural production of what became the Marlowe Society

17

which is still widely known for its performances of Elizabethan plays. Justin Brooke, the most experienced actor in the company, played Faustus, Rupert Mephistopheles.

Even more important for him was the next Marlowe venture, a production of *Comus* as part of Christ College's celebration in 1908 of the Milton Tercentenary. As the Attendant Spirit he was said by one reviewer to be 'the best of the performers, and a better reciter of blank verse than we have heard of late anywhere'. Francis Cornford (a Fellow of Trinity, later to be Laurence Professor of Ancient Philosophy) played Comus, and the beginnings of Rupert's friendship with him and more especially with Frances Darwin whom Cornford was shortly to marry, date from then. It was revolutionary in the Cambridge of that time for women to be involved in a production, as were not only Frances but her cousin Gwen Darwin, later to marry a French painter, Jacques Raverat, and to achieve distinction both as a wood-engraver and as author of *Period Piece*. Gwen was fellow seamstress with Ka Cox, of whom more later.

Apart from taking a major rôle in *Comus*, Rupert seemed at one time to be carrying much of its organization on his Rugby head-of-house shoulders. But it was the preparatory work on the text which chiefly interested him, and he studied everything from theatre construction to textual criticism. The experience deepened his devotion to Milton's poetry (he told Frances Cornford that when he took a volume of Milton from the shelf he found his hand trembling to think what was in it); it deepened his interest in drama and music; and, as Edward Dent was later to recall, it assisted the development of an ideal, ever present in his mind, of 'young Cambridge, as the source from which the most vital movements in literature, art, and drama were to spring'.

The ideal of young Cambridge was the theme of a reflective letter from Bertrand Russell, who had just read Marsh's *Memoir*, to Lady Ottoline Morrell. Marsh 'goes building up the respectable legend', and it makes Russell 'very sad and very indignant'.

> It hurts reading of all that young world swept away – Rupert and his brother and Keeling and lots of others – in whom one foolishly thought at the time that there was hope for the world – they were full of life and energy and truth . . .

Russell had come to know Rupert well on his election in 1908 to the Apostles. Marsh, himself an Apostle, wrote of 'that old, great, secret, but vaguely famous Brotherhood from which the membership of Tennyson and others of the illustrious has lifted a corner of the veil'.

More recently the membership of Anthony Blunt and other thirties communists has lifed further corners; but the presiding spirit in Brooke's day was the philosopher, G. E. Moore. Geoffrey Keynes's elder brother, the economist Maynard (later Lord) Keynes, was to recall Moore's influence upon himself and his contemporaries. His *Principia Ethica* (1903) was 'not only overwhelming; . . . it was exciting, exhilarating, the beginning of a renaissance, the opening of a new heaven on a new earth, we were the forerunners of a new dispensation, we were not afraid of anything'. Rupert's papers to the Society (unpublished save for 'A or B?' which I included in my earlier selection of his work) show his concern with Moore's question of 'what was good in itself' and acceptance of his conclusion that metaphysics, 'as the investigation of a supposed supersensible reality', had no logical bearing on the answer. What mattered were 'states of mind' and which of them were good or bad, a question which seemed to depend finally on one's intuition. In company with fellow Apostles such as Keynes, E. M. Forster and Lytton Strachey, Rupert seemed to share little of the philosophical spirit Moore was eager to foster, and seized rather upon the incidental answers he provided: 'We accepted Moore's religion, so to speak, and discarded his morals', said Keynes. But it is interesting to see from his papers how a sensitive, intelligent man of the time could respond to the limitations of the *Principia* and look forward in his own thinking to Sartre and Existentialism before even the works of Kierkegaard had become known in English.

The Frederick (Ben) Keeling mentioned by Russell was in his third year at Trinity when he had (in Hugh Dalton's own word) 'netted' him for the Cambridge Fabians. Dalton, who was Rupert's contemporary at King's, recalled with a youthful enthusiasm he retained throughout his life how he and Rupert and their friends thought of their generation as far superior to any that had preceded it, a sentiment no less apparent in Keynes and Russell. He always claimed that the lines from 'Second Best':

> Yet, behind the night,
> Waits for the great unborn, somewhere afar,
> Some white tremendous daybreak

foretold the dawning of a socialist state; and he linked them with a giant poster in Ben Keeling's rooms which depicted the workers of the world surging forward with clenched fists, and under it the legend: 'Forward, the day is breaking'. Rupert became an associate member of the Cambridge Fabians in 1907, a full member in 1908, and its President in

19

1909, being one of the most effective in its history. It was said that, if one chanced to meet him when there was talk of an industrial dispute, he would be as well versed in the complications of social questions as in the obscurities of Donne.

In 'Democracy and the Arts', a paper which he delivered to the Fabians on 24 November 1910, he examined the situation – 'and remember it's a real one' – in which art is important, the people who produce it are nearly all dependent on unearned incomes, and 'we are going to diminish and extinguish the number of those [so] dependent.' His argument and solution, in part prophetic of the Arts Council, may still have some currency. In a letter of the same day E. M. Forster wrote to him: 'I have this moment decided to put all I can remember of your paper on art into a novel – and as I remember it.' The novel was the unfinished *Arctic Summer*, first published in 1980. The paper itself was published in February 1947 when Hugh Dalton was Chancellor of the Exchequer. It contains, wrote Dalton in *Call Back Yesterday* (1953), 'some suggestions, still worth considering, for a Socialist policy for the encouragement of artists'. Forster reviewed it warmly for the B.B.C. (Eastern Service, 12 March 1947), concluding his talk:

> Had Brooke lived, . . . he would certainly have become a live wire in public affairs, and an energetic and enlightened administrator. He had the necessary mixture of toughness and idealism.

Neither at Rugby nor at Cambridge were the Classics first among Rupert's interests. His Second in the Classical Tripos was none the less a disappointment. Hassall suggests and Lehmann repeats that it was debated whether his papers did not more properly belong to a still lower class; but Frances Cornford recalled that her husband, who was more ready to judge work by its quality than its quantity, had recommended him for a First. When his supervisor suggested that he should give up the Classics and concentrate on English literature, he eagerly concurred. Acting also on his advice that he should retreat from the social life of Cambridge which was beginning to overwhelm him, he took lodgings at Grantchester, first at the Orchard, and in the following year at the Old Vicarage next door. He claimed that he did not really begin to live until he went out of College: it was his first real escape from institutional life.

In his first term at Grantchester he worked for the Charles Oldham Shakespeare scholarship which he won with his first essay on Webster. He spent the Lent term as acting housemaster of School Field following the death of his father on the eve of the school's return. Back in Grantchester for the Easter term, he worked on a study of 'Puritanism as Represented or Referred to in the Early English Drama up to 1642', with which he won the Harness Prize. It was after spending three months in Munich that he returned to the Old Vicarage, a far more tumbled-down old house than one sees now – in the interests of preservation the Jeffrey Archers have gutted it – with what was then a wild garden, a labyrinth of flowers and weeds in which he walked 'like a fly crawling on the score of the Fifth Symphony'. He always felt most at home in wild surroundings; and once, on visiting a more formal garden in which white lilies were displayed against a green and silver background of fig-tree boughs, he felt uncomfortable, 'as if the Angel Gabriel might pop out at any moment and announce something.'

His chief work during the latter part of 1911 was a fellowship dissertation on 'John Webster and the Elizabethan Drama' which he finished with difficulty (he gained the fellowship on a second attempt in 1913). He appeared as a negro slave in *The Magic Flute*, and scribbled hard in a dressing-room when not wanted on stage. He was preparing his *Poems*, and in brief intervals of Webster corresponded with his publisher, 'who's always discovering new indecencies . . . and demanding omissions'. When they appeared in December, he wrote:

> I've an insistent queer feeling of having got rid of poems I've written and published – of having cut the umbilical chord – that they're now just slightly more anybody's concern than mine, and that everybody else has an equal right and a faintly greater opportunity of understanding them.

He elsewhere confessed to feeling 'that degrading ecstasy that I have always despised in parents whose shapeless offspring are praised for beauty'.

Some of the early poems, such as 'The Hill', were written about and for Rupert's first love, Noel Olivier. Up to the time of her death (in April 1969), Dr Noel Olivier Richards steadfastly refused publication of his letters to her in the collection which Geoffrey Keynes had long been preparing, even though she seems at one time to have considered their separate publication. Without them, and those to her three sisters, it is difficult to judge the importance of their relationship. Her father, Sir Sydney (later Lord) Olivier, had been invited to address the Cambridge Fabians in May 1907. It was at a supper party in Ben Keeling's rooms before the meeting that Rupert first met Noel, then a girl of fifteen and a half and still at school at Bedales. They were to meet frequently over several years, often in secret, and were for a time unofficially 'engaged'. Their last known meeting was five months before his death.

Of far greater consequence was Rupert's love for Katharine Cox, known to all her friends as Ka. While still a child she had lost her mother, and shared with her elder sister responsibility for the home and family: a younger sister and a stockbroker father of radical views to whom she was devoted. Her father's death in 1905, the year before she went up to Newnham, was an emotional deprivation from which she never fully recovered. She and Rupert, who was by four months her junior, met during their first year at Cambridge. They were fellow members of the Fabians, one of whose revolutionary achievements, like that of the Marlowe Society, was to break down barriers between men's and women's colleges. Ka was plain but evidently attractive, warm and motherly in her affections, and wide in her sympathies. 'To be with her', said Frances Cornford, 'was like sitting in a green field of clover . . . She accepted everybody without criticism, and then gave out, not knowing how much she was giving.' It was no doubt a craving for that 'sleepy mother-comfort' he writes of in 'A Memory' that led Rupert after several years of friendship to look upon her with a different feeling. When Jacques Raverat, with whom she had been in 'a sort of fast-and-loose state', became engaged to Gwen, she became very upset; and when Jacques and Gwen married she felt deserted and threw herself upon Rupert, who said he loved Noel. But his full passion seems first to have been roused by jealousy.

The occasion was a reading party at Lulworth late in December 1911. Two days after Christmas Rupert arrived at lodgings with Lytton Strachey, other members of the party, including Ka, being accommodated nearby. The painter Henry Lamb joined them on the afternoon of the 30th. What followed, though confused, has usually been told from Rupert's side. Here is what Lamb's recent biographer, Keith Clements, reports:

> Henry decided Ka was far the nicest there and lightheartedly flirted with her, greatly to the upset and annoyance of Rupert who, over that week-end, became insanely jealous, literally to the point of breakdown. Not only did he think Henry guilty of ruining his chances with Ka but suspected Lytton of being a party to the plot.

The last seems a particularly strange imputation of Rupert's, since he was well aware of Strachey's homosexual preferences and almost certainly aware of his love for Lamb. Lamb himself – 'for once', says his biographer – seems to have been innocent of any conscious effort to inflame the situation. When Rupert, beside himself and in desperation, asked Ka to marry him, she told him she was in love with Lamb.

Subsequently, as we learn from Strachey's biographer, Michael Holroyd, Lytton wrote to Lamb that 'I almost believe the best thing she [Ka] could do now would be to marry Rupert straight off', and two days later he tells him that he 'ought to reflect a good deal before letting her become your mistress'. But Rupert was not to know all this.

We may accept the conjecture of Hassall, fairly based if delicately understated, that it was 'natural for idealistic love, poisoned by jealous fears, to ascribe the motives of a libertine to its prospering rival.' Rupert was his mother's son, and nowhere is the Ranee's puritanism more evident than in his jealous, protective urge to keep Ka unspotted by the world. Many of his letters from this time forth speak of a revulsion from dirtiness, a hunger for cleanness. The pedagogic tone ('Am I the mere schoolmaster-clergyman? One's *anything* when one's in love and in pain') expressed itself in fearful warnings and injunctions both to her and to their mutual friends. Even the published extracts from his letters are painful witness to the confusion, revulsion, self-loathing which were to result from this emotional crisis.

Rupert left Lulworth on the verge of a breakdown. A London nerve specialist prescribed complete rest. The accommodating Ka agreed to be his companion in Munich. Meanwhile he joined the Ranee in an hotel in Cannes, writing almost daily to Ka, and escaping by subterfuge after three weeks to join her in Verona and travel thence to Munich. She was not in love with him; she believed herself to be in love with Lamb. She nursed him as lovingly as any mother – he was still in a pitiful state of health – and for a time he seemed to regain health and weight. They were living together now as lovers; and she chose what she thought was the right moment – it was when they were leaving Munich in mid-February for a week-end on the Starnberger See – to confess that, while he had been pouring out his feelings to her from Cannes, she had been continuing to see Lamb. His reaction was fiercer than she could have anticipated. He relapsed into the state in which she had seen him in Lulworth less than two months previously. Four days later they cut short their stay and returned hurriedly to England.

Rupert was shocked and humiliated to think that Ka should have allowed herself to be loved by him while her true affections were elsewhere. She, who had acted out of pity and compassion, one might say therapeutically, became now the victim of passionate resentment. From the South Seas ('Waikiki') he was to write:

> Of two that loved – or did not love – and one
> Whose perplexed heart did evil, foolishly,
> A long while since, and by some other sea.

23

As he fell out of love with her – fell at first into a sort of deadness of feeling – so, with the perversity of human nature, she found herself falling in love with him. There were trials and failures, forgivenesses and reconciliations. From this time, it seems, Rupert could never again feel sure of his love for any woman. 'You see', he wrote to her in the autumn of 1912, 'I fell in love again with Noel . . . So it was bad with me when it appeared how utterly she had fallen out of love with me. I felt I *couldn't* live.' It may be said here that many of his friends were worried by his talk of suicide. Desperately at times as he longed for marriage, and longed for children ('Their sons, they gave, their immortality'), and widely as he loved and was loved, he could never commit himself. In another letter to Ka he wrote: 'I'm somehow rotten. And I guess it will be better if I don't leave children – people like me – behind.'

In his paranoia – the word is not too strong: even the discreet and loyal Geoffrey Keynes allows that 'he seemed to his friends to be almost out of his mind' – he broke not only with Lytton Strachey but with his brother James and others of his Bloomsbury friends. 'It is not inconceivable', writes Lehmann, 'that what really upset him was a hidden fear that Lytton and his friends thought that he was more attracted by his own rather than the other sex.' 'Pure sodomy', he said in an unpublished paper on Shakespeare, 'is a pretty affectation in the young, but if it is anything more, leads to second-rateness, sentimentality, fluff, gentle dilettante slush.' How near he himself may once have been to the intellectual decision to become a passive homosexual is suggested by his later vehemence against 'hermaphroditism' as he called it. But in the end it revolted him, and he turned from it with the same puritanical hardness with which he cut Lytton Strachey dead, in public, in the foyer at Drury Lane.

Among all his friends, no-one was more understanding than Frances Cornford. To her in particular he confided his feelings about Ka, and she did most by her loving concern for each of them to console and reassure. She it was who suggested that Rupert should get away from it all for a year by going to America. Almost a year was to pass before his acceptance of this good advice and his sailing for America in May 1913. From then until his return in June 1914 was the most productive period of his life. Many of his finest poems were written when he could, like John Donne, distance himself from his experiences. The letters to his friends are among the best as the Keynes collection is sufficient witness. The articles he wrote for the *Westminster Gazette*, published later as *Letters from America*, read freshly and amusingly to this day. From such a wealth of documentation I shall not attempt to select for this brief outline of his life. This only, from a letter to Cathleen Nesbitt, the young actress whom he had met in December 1912 and 'adored' thereafter, must speak for the happiness he found in the South Seas:

> Will it come to your having to fetch me? The boat's ready to start; the brown lovely people in their bright clothes are gathered on the old wharf to wave her away. Everyone has a white flower behind their ears. Mamua has given me one. Do you know the significance of a white flower worn over the ear? A white flower over the right ear means 'I am looking for a sweetheart.' And a white flower over the left ear means 'I have found a sweetheart.' And a white flower over each ear means 'I have found one sweetheart, and am looking for another.' A white flower over each ear, my dear, is dreadfully the most fashionable way of adorning yourself in Tahiti.

How prophetically had he written in a manuscript note of 1906: 'The life of a poet is made up of tragedies: they begin with an infatuation and end with a sonnet sequence'! In Tahiti, where he spent three months, he met the Mamua of 'Tiare Tahiti', a native girl of Mataia called Taatamata, who became his mistress. A letter from her, which had lain for several months in the wreck of the *Empress of Ireland*, reached him in January 1915, and is included as a footnote in the Keynes *Letters*.

On his return there were two happy months spent mostly in London, with Eddie Marsh as master of many ceremonies. Two days before the declaration of war, he wrote to Marsh:

> I *did* enjoy July. It's now a far and lovely vision. . . . Do you have a Brussels-before-Waterloo feeling that we'll all – or some – meet with other eyes in 1915?

He was staying with the Cornfords in Cley, Norfolk, when war was declared. The article which he wrote for the *New Statesman*, 'An Unusual Young Man', is not at all representative of his best despite its selection for *The Oxford Book of English Prose*. It seems both to over-simplify and over-dramatize what were more complex and less consistent feelings. But a fuller understanding of his personal difficulties and his acute sense that, far from being 'a panorama of earth's loveliest experiences', his life had been a failure, would show in retrospect that the war came as a release for him (see 'Peace'), a return to 'Nobleness' ('The Dead'). 'Well,' says the Unusual Young Man, 'if Armageddon's *on*, I suppose one should be there.'

Edward Marsh was private secretary to Winston Churchill; Rupert was offered a commission in Churchill's newly formed Royal Naval Division. After a brief training, he was sent on October 4 on an abortive expedition to relieve Antwerp, which gave him his only first-hand experience of war. Of the Belgian refugees he wrote:

> I'll never forget that white-faced, endless procession in the night, pressed aside to let the military – us – pass, crawling forward at some hundred yards an hour, quite hopeless, the old men crying, and the women with hard drawn faces.

He was strengthened in his resolve:

> . . . apart from the tragedy – I've never felt happier or better in my life than in those days in Belgium. . . . I know that whatever happens, I'll be doing some good, fighting to prevent *that*.

After two days spent mostly in the trenches, came the withdrawal, and the Division started on its homeward march in conditions of great hardship.

The '1914' sonnets had been partly in mind before the Antwerp expedition. The first tentative jottings of four of them were made in a small field-notebook, interspersed among notes from military lectures: 'Every officer should be easily found', 'German explosive shells carry further back than forward', 'Keep *strict* discipline'. It is well that the beginnings of these idealistic sonnets should be thus preserved among tokens of more practical concern. Even though he finished them after the experience of Antwerp, on leave in late December, they were poems, not of war, but of preparation for war. Many of the thoughts and phrases in them reflect what was 'in the air' at the time. It is doubtful whether he would have read the reactionary *Morning Post*, let alone have been influenced by the naïve sentiments expressed in its leaders, but there are parallels in them. Expressions that 'manly animosities of war' are preferable to the sloth, selfishness and cowardice of 'a shameful peace' ('. . . war is not altogether an evil: it cleans and purifies: it invigorates . . .'), that 'the soul of England is the soul of the sum of Englishmen living and dead', and that all people are 'parts of a great whole, whose destiny and interest are of infinitely higher importance than their own' – all these are exactly reflected in the sonnets.

It is also well to remember that the feelings of those two poets who, more vividly than any, were to express the later mood of disillusion, were very different in the early months. Wilfred Owen at the outset felt a sense of 'new crusade and modern knightliness'. In the summer of 1915, shortly after Rupert Brooke's death, Siegfried Sassoon could write in 'Absolution':

> The anguish of the earth absolves our eyes
> Till beauty shines in all that we can see.
> War is our scourge; yet war has made us wise,
> And, fighting for our freedom, we are free.

On 1 March 1915 the Hood Battallion of the Royal Naval Division embarked at Avonmouth bound for the Dardanelles. 'I've never been so happy in my life', he wrote; and realized suddenly that 'the ambition of my life has been – since I was two – to go on a military expedition against Constantinople.' But he was never to see action there, and most of his friends and fellow officers were to die in that ill-fated expedition. The actual cause of Rupert's death was septicaemia when he was still weak from the effects of heatstroke and dysentery. But such unglamorous details were deemed inappropriate by the obituarists and propagandists of the time. The most famous of the '1914' sonnets, 'The Soldier', had been quoted in St Paul's on Easter Sunday by its 'gloomy Dean', W.R. Inge. *The Times* of April 5 reported the sermon, and gave the sonnet in full. The *Cambridge Magazine* (ironically, one day after Rupert's death) included a précis of the sermon:

> The enthusiasm of a pure and elevated patriotism, free from hate and bitterness, and fear, had never found a nobler expression. And yet it fell somewhat short of Isaiah's vision and still more of the Christian hope.

Rupert received a cutting from *The Times*. His last recorded remark was a regret that the Dean hadn't thought him as good as Isaiah.

In *The Times* of exactly three weeks later there was no such reservation in the rolling tones with which Winston Churchill commemorated his death:

> During the last few months of his life, months of preparation in gallant comradeship and open air, the poet-soldier told with all the simple force of genius the sorrow of youth about to die. . . .
> Joyous, fearless, versatile, deeply instructed, with classic symmetry of mind and body, he was all that one would wish England's noblest sons to be in days when no sacrifice but the most precious is acceptable, and the most precious is that which is most freely proffered.

The most fitting memorial was composed by Rupert himself in the fragment of an elegy. Hassall, Lehmann and I (in my earlier

conclude our accounts of the life with the lines, and I will do
ain:

> He wears
> The ungathered blossom of quiet; stiller he
> Than a deep well at noon, or lovers met;
> Than sleep, or the heart after wrath. He is
> The silence following great words of peace.

3 THE POEMS

Rupert Brooke was from the first a deliberate poet. His earliest verse,
written at the age of ten after seeing a great wave break over the sea-
front, was fashioned according to his newly acquired knowledge that
blank verse should have five feet with two beats in each foot. Here is the
remarkable last line:

> One day Poseidon grown strong will conquer.

He seems always to have needed the discipline of a metrical form. He
rejected free verse, and wrote in a review of Ezra Pound's *Personae*: 'It is
certain (thanks in part to Mr Saintsbury) that the foot is immensely
important in English prosody. It is still more certain that the line is.' In
an earlier review he had chided the President of Magdalen College,
Oxford, T. H. Warren, for his metrics in *The Death of Virgil*: 'The
blank verse is pedantic, but not from lack of licence. Several lines have a
foot too many.' D. H. Lawrence accused Edward Marsh of being 'a bit of
a policeman in poetry'; he might have said likewise of his fellow
Georgian.

Brooke would often speak of the difficulties facing a poet who was
anxious to study the technique of his craft. For any other art one could
have found a school where certain rules were taught and methodical criticism offered. As his only course he constantly sought good models.
'He had read everything', wrote Virginia Woolf, 'and he had read it
from the point of view of a working writer . . . His judgements were not
only very definite but had a freedom and reality which mark the criticism of those who are themselves working in the same art . . . To work
hard, much harder than most writers think it necessary, was an injunc-
tion that remains in memory.'

Evidence of the hard work and an indication of his methods of com-
position can be found in his notebooks. One of them, dating from
his Grantchester days, begins with notes on the structure of poems he
has been reading. These are followed by lists of words such as 'syllabub',

'paravent', 'postule' from the poems of Browning; 'arval-bread = baked-meats' (see Ambarvalia'), 'queasy' (see 'Jealousy'). Words were 'absolute symbols' for him, said Walter de la Mare; 'They mean precisely what they say and only what they say.' Whereas de la Mare found words to be 'obstinate and artificial symbols' – a restriction upon expression, he once said, rather than a means of it – words were for Brooke not only a means of expression but sometimes the motive for it. 'Oh, it sets me singing', is his mocking response to news that Marsh has torn a ligament. 'Isn't ligature – or is it ligament? – a lovely word?

> Is it prudent? is it Pure?
> To go and break a ligature?

'A word is an idea with an atmosphere', he wrote in his dissertation on Webster, 'a hard core with a fringe round it, like an oyster with a beard . . . Poets think of the fringes.'

In the same notebook he transcribes passages from his reading, chiefly from the letters of Shelley, but also from Keats, Shakespeare, Dryden and Yeats. In his dissertation he wrote about Webster's use of notebooks with a sympathy born of his own practice: 'A man tends to collect quotations, phrases, and ideas, that particularly appeal to and fit in with his own personality.' He belonged, like Webster, to 'the caddis-worm school of writers, who do not become their complete selves until they are encrusted with a thousand orts and chips and fragments from the world around.' 'Originality', he writes earlier in the same work, 'is only plagiarising from a great many.' Although not – except perhaps in this sense – a plagiarist, Brooke practised what Ben Jonson held to be 'the third requisite in our poet, or maker', the art of 'Imitation'.

It would be wrong to suggest, however, that he depended on literary stimuli for his poems. As his notebooks show, the poems begin by his 'collecting a few words, detaching lines from the ambient air', or – I quote from one of his last letters – 'collaring one or two golden phrases that a certain wind blows from (will the Censor let me say?) Olympus, across these purple seas'. The notebooks show how these phrases were pieced together, amplified, modified, with blanks left for the unforthcoming words, so that the manuscript at this stage might resemble a jigsaw puzzle with pieces missing from it. The manner in which one of these pieces was supplied has been recorded by Leonard Woolf. 'At one moment he said: ''Virginia, what is the brightest thing you can think of?'' ''A leaf with the light on it'', was Virginia's instant reply.' And a blank space towards the end of 'Town and Country' was filled in immediately:

> Cloud-like we lean and stare as bright leaves stare.

An interesting example of the later stages of Brooke's 'carpentry' is given in the *Memoir*, where Marsh prints the first and final drafts of the 'Psychical Research' sonnet. Hassall is more ambitious in printing drafts of 'Seaside' with a conjectural commentary.

There was one weakness in the course of apprenticeship Brook prescribed for himself, though it was less his fault than of the times. It would be hard to imagine more unfortunate models for a young poet than Swinburne and the poets of the decadent nineties whom his wish for 'modernism' embraced – unless, one is tempted to add, it be Brooke himself as reflected in the juvenilia of his disciples. Like Swinburne, he never quite succeeded in fusing body and soul, which is one reason why, as Patric Dickinson has suggested, he appeals to adolescence 'eternally caught in the same predicament'. And just as his disciples have been most enamoured of the 'red mournful roses', the 'little creeping shadows', the 'white lips of desire', so he too fell victim to Swinburne's and Dowson's worst excesses. He never entirely outgrew his inclination to 'load every rift with ore'; and a facetious entry in the same Grantchester notebook from which I have quoted:

> . . . twittered the epithalamion of day and darkness, and the occident was scarlet with hymeneal flames

shows that such loading of the rifts, though he might reject them critically, continued to hold a fascination for him.

In a paper on 'Modern Poetry' he commended Dowson to the Rugby sixth form. Quoting Victor Hugo's remark to Baudelaire, 'You have created a new shudder', he suggested one might say of Dowson, 'He has created a new sigh'. There are many sighs among Brooke's juvenilia. The Dowsonian alexandrines of 'Day that I have loved' and the obvious link between 'Dead Men's Love' and Dowson's 'Amor Profanus' are further evidence of discipleship. St John Lucas, whose encouragement of 'decadence' has been mentioned, seems to have been more directly implicated in the sonnets 'Menelaus and Helen', for he wrote in a novel which Brooke admired that 'Helen became a bald and withered hag' and 'Menelaus was palsied and querulous, and was ever upbraiding her'.

The earliest of Brooke's poems to suggest his better later work is the sonnet 'Seaside'. The lines in the sestet:

> . . . In the deep heart of me
> The sullen waters swell towards the moon,
> And all my tides set seaward . . .

look forward to that remarkable line from one of the last fragments:

> In Avons of the heart her rivers run.

But in another sense the poem looks backward to a more profitable influence; and the new note appears in two slightly later sonnets:

> When the high session of the day is ended
>
> ('Day and Night')

> Such long swift tides stir not a land-locked sea
> (Sonnet, 'I said I splendidly loved you')

Brooke, it is clear, was working now on the Elizabethans. In 'Dust' he builds on an idea from Cowley's 'All-over Love':

> Hereafter if one *Dust* of me
>   Mixt with anothers *Substance* be,
> 'Twill *Leaven* that whole *Lump* with Love of thee.
>   Let Nature if she please disperse
> My *Atoms* over all the Universe,
>   At the last they eas'ly shall
>   Themselves know, and together call;
> For thy Love, like a *Mark*, is stamp'd on all.

If it is true that Swinburne is still present in 'Dust' (and Shelley, in the epithet 'swift' applied to a woman's hair), such words as 'dance', 'gleam', 'eager', 'sweet', 'radiant', 'flame' and 'ecstasy' serve now to enliven and give warmth to the calculated metaphysics of Cowley. In some of the verses, from the fourth verse to the seventh, there is a suggestion of the unforced lyrical quality of the best of his later poems, 'Retrospect' and 'Tiare Tahiti'.

When W. B. Yeats said that, 'if Brooke could rid his poems of a "languid sensualness", he would probably become a very great poet', he was speaking before these later poems had appeared. F. R. Leavis, in the context of a less favourable comment, wrote of 'a certain original talent' and 'a genuine sensuousness rather like Keats's (though more energetic) and something that is rather like Keats's vulgarity' – for it was Keats, of course, who had urged Shelley to ' ''load every rift'' of your subject with ore'. Yeats's 'languid' might aptly refer to the pre-Raphaelite 'Ante Aram'; Leavis's 'energetic', which more truly suggests Brooke's character, is more apt to the later poems. In these the prevailing influence is of John Donne.

James Elroy Flecker called Brooke 'our Donne Redivivus'. Here was a poet with whose love poems at least he could feel in close sympathy, and the two essays he wrote on him in 1913 are excellent introductions to his own poetry as well as to Donne's. One could point to instances of particular indebtedness: to the obvious connexion between 'Heaven' and Donne's 'The Baite'; to his borrowing in 'Beauty and Beauty' the epithet 'scattering-bright' from 'Aire and Angels'; to his direct quotation from 'The Anniversarie' in 'Safety'. But Donne's influence is more subtle, more pervasive. We sense it in the wit, the humour, the irony, the love of paradox, the tougher intellectual qualities of the later poems. 'Brooke mocked at the things – people, places and ideas alike – that he loved most tenderly, and loved the things he laughed at', said Frances Cornford. And with his poems, as with Donne's, 'at any given moment . . . it is often impossible to discern which he is doing most'.

It is easy to point to other influences: to the Milton of 'L'Allegro' in 'Grantchester'; to Drayton's 'The Parting' in 'The Chilterns'; to Marvell's 'A Dialogue between the Soul and Body' in the 'Psychical Research' sonnet; to Meredith's 'Modern Love' sonnet 16 in 'The Hill', and to the idea of Meredith's whole sequence in Brooke's love sonnets from the South Seas. But we do not read Brooke's poems as an anthology of other poets. Increasingly he was finding his own voice; to hear it one requires not commentary so much as freshness of response.

'There is no one the least like him', wrote Harold Monro on Brooke's death. 'No one has his frankness, no one his ingenuity, his incisiveness, or his humour.' There is something in the physical toughness of the poems, in their muscularity, which is such as to make one sense the presence of the man within the verse. Walter de la Mare called his writing, both in verse and prose, 'a kind of action'.

Although Brooke admired Donne's humour, his humour is peculiarly his own. There was a strain of the sentimental in him which, in the early poems especially, he indulged, finding ample precedents among the decadent writers. Even then, however, he could stand back and mock himself in his borrowed robes. When first he reacted against the sentimental, he did so with a studied fierceness: 'So far the poet . . .'. In later poems he would check the worst excesses by the half-conscious play of humour. Only in the '1914' sonnets is there no trace of that. In them, as Edward Dent first said and others have echoed, the romanticism he so much dreaded came uppermost.

Above all Brooke's poems are charged with and surrender that 'individual and bewildering ghost', his personality. 'They seem as we read them', said de la Mare, 'to bring us into a happy, instant relationship with him.' They are free from those defensive barriers which poets so often build:

> When you were there, and you, and you . . .

> I think if you had loved me when I wanted . . .

> These I have loved . . .

He assumed, and with a disarming sincerity, that his own fortunes must be nearest his readers' hearts; we cannot read him with detachment. 'A man's poetry', wrote H. W. Garrod, 'is, after all, only one part of his greatness; and indeed, only one part of his poetry.'

4 THEIR PLACE

Apart from the predictable reaction against the '1914' sonnets, there was in the years following the First World War a reaction against all things Georgian. In *Georgian Poetry 1912–1922* I have traced the history of a movement which, though fortuitous and informal in its inception, more or less casual and entirely untheoretical, came to represent for later generations a literary establishment of the most reactionary kind. Instead of marking all forty of those poets whom Edward Marsh anthologized with a Georgian ranch-brand, it would be more appropriate to consider the variety, independence and distinction of many of them: Edmund Blunden, W. H. Davies, Walter de la Mare, J. E. Flecker, Robert Graves, Ralph Hodgson, D. H. Lawrence, John Masefield, Harold Monro, Isaac Rosenberg, Siegfried Sassoon, James Stephens make a round dozen; add Rupert Brooke – not least among them – for a baker's.

The poet, novelist and critic John Wain, writing in 1972, argued that, 'if the First World War had not happened, the new idiom in English poetry would have been a development of Georgianism.'

> The seeds were there: the honesty, the dislike of cant, the 'selection from the real language of men', the dissatisfaction with a narrow tradition of poetry laid down by the literary Establishment. . . .

He cites Edward Thomas and Wilfred Owen as major poets who 'take off from Georgianism'.

> If their flight had been longer, there would have been no need for a modern poetic idiom imported from France via America . . . Owen and Thomas, abetted by the excellent poets who survived the war, by Graves, by Blunden, by the older poets like Hodgson and de la Mare, would have made a living tradition out of English materials arising naturally from English life. If they had, the Auden generation, coming into a healthier situation, might have developed differently, and better.

As we know, however, the publication of the fifth *Georgian Poetry* anthology in 1922 coincided with the appearance of Eliot's 'The Waste Land'. And W. H. Auden was to write:

> For gasworks and dried tubers, I foresook
> The clock at Grantchester, the English rook.

It may help in reassessing Brooke's place in English poetry to remember that one of the Americans to whom Wain alludes, Ezra Pound, wrote of him as 'the best of all that Georgian group' (of whom, incidentally, he too would have been a member had the poems Marsh asked for been available); and that the other, T. S. Eliot, admired at least one of Brooke's poems, 'The Fish', and seems to have had 'Grantchester' in mind in the opening lines of 'The Waste Land'. In his early poems Eliot shared Brooke's fascination with the disgusting and his delight in polysyllables for satirical effect (*c.f.* Brooke's 'Intolerable consanguinity' with Eliot's 'Polyphiloprogenitive'). Brooke's Smet-Smet, the Hippopotamus Goddess, would seem to have some 'consanguinity' with Eliot's 'broad-backed Hippopotamus', the Established Church. Again, as G. S. Fraser observed, we are sometimes struck by imagery in Brooke's poems that 'seems to foretell a coming shift of taste:

> Heart, you are restless as a paper scrap
>   That's tossed down dusty pavements by the wind.

This was the sort of thing Eliot would notice.'

It is not at all my purpose to argue that Brooke would or could have been another Eliot. What he might have done, whether as a poet, or (as E. M. Forster thought) a prose writer, or (as Virginia Woolf suggested) a prime minister, it is pointless now to speculate. Equally it is pointless to dismiss him as of little consequence because he was a Georgian, or a pre-Owen 'war poet', or 'the most beautiful young man in England'. He was a poet of considerable promise and some achievement. He should be read anew.

5 THE TEXT

This makes no claim to be a scholarly edition of the poems of Rupert Brooke, but I have taken pains to make it a reliable one. I have consulted both the Marsh and Keynes editions and other printed texts as well as many of the manuscripts. Like Keynes, I have not disturbed the minor changes made by his first editor, 'no one being better able to interpret Brooke's mind'. Only in one place have I taken a liberty which Marsh considered but did not take, preferring 'noons are lost in endless day' in 'Tiare Tahiti' to 'moons' which is in the manuscript. I have followed Keynes in his two emendations to 'The Night Journey' authorized by a fair copy of the poem now in the Rupert Brooke archive in King's College. Despite some reservations, I have also followed him in his dating of the poems.

In the *Poems* of 1911, the only book of his to be published in his lifetime, Brooke arranged the poems in three sections: poems of 1908–1911, experiments ('Choriambics' I and II, and 'Desertion'), and poems of 1905–1908. This enabled him to place at the end such slighter poems as 'The Beginning' (Keynes dates it as 1907, and according to his dating only 'The Song of the Beasts' of 1906 is earlier) and to begin with some of his later and better. Though the sections themselves were in reverse chronology, he allowed himself freedom within them. Thus the sonnet 'Oh! Death will find me' of April 1909 is placed first (in all likelihood because it referred to Noel to whom he had offered dedication of the book, which she had refused). In his 'second edition revised' of the *Collected Poems* (1928) Edward Marsh noted that, while Brooke's practice had been followed hitherto, 'the better way is to begin at the beginning, and [the poems] now appear, as far as possible, in the sequence in which they were written.' Curiously, although the order of the sections is reversed, the poems within each section are in identical order.

Marsh was careful of Brooke's reputation in his selection for the *Collected Poems*, and added only two to their number subsequently, 'Fafaïa' and 'It's not going to happen again', each having appeared posthumously in the *London Mercury*. In the Preface to *The Poetical Works* of 1946, Keynes claims that 'the 82 poems of the original two volumes have been increased to 120': in fact, the 94 poems of the Marsh edition have been increased by the 26 poems as listed by Keynes himself in his *Bibliography*. But even 26 additions seem excessive. Nor would his claim that 'when a poet has passed his third decade of posthumous fame and has come to be accepted as a national possession, his early efforts acquire an interest for the evidence they afford of the influences at work during formative years' seem justification for most of them, juvenilia which Brooke himself rejected for the 1911 *Poems*. It follows that I have not included these. I had at first intended to be more rigorous in excluding poems from the Marsh edition; but, one by one, many of them made their claim – for a line here, for a biographical comment there, or, in the case of 'Second Best', for that possible political meaning which Dalton suggested.

Lest it should then seem perverse to have added poems which both the poet and his other editors rejected, I must offer my own justification. I do not pretend that any of the additions represents Brooke at his best, or even second best, but I would claim that each adds something of interest to what is already known. Both Marsh and Keynes considered the 'Epilogue in Heaven' for inclusion, and Marsh indeed printed it in *A Number of People* (1939), acclaiming it with justice 'a delightful thing'. The 'Fragment' from a strange hymn in which geometrical expressions are treated as Platonic Ideas was printed in Hassall's *Rupert Brooke* (p. 292) but, oddly, without its best couplet: though probably earlier in date, it seems to belong with 'Heaven'. The 'Sicilian Octave' was the first of his poems to be printed in the *Westminster Gazette* whose weekly competitions, later continued in the *Saturday Westminster*, gave him practice in his craft; it is a notable example of the deliberateness I have mentioned. The translation of Horace was written in the school text he used at Rugby. The translation of Christian Wagner was composed, before he knew German, from a literal version provided by Geoffrey Keynes; it was to win his second prize in the *Westminster*, and was the subject of the entertaining 'Comment' I have printed as an appendix to it. 'Hymm 666', the lines 'Under a picture of a schoolmaster', the 'Ballade' for James Strachey, and the stanza from the 'Ballade of Middle Age', have never before been printed. They are a few among many examples in manuscript of his ability to dash off light verse for an occasion, and seem better as such than most of those printed in Hassall's biography or *The Letters*.

Brooke was an uneven poet, and his best is not always helped by the proximity of the less good. I have hoped that, by separating the better poems from the (chiefly) juvenilia, the progress from 'Seaside' through the poems from the South Seas to the moving last fragments may show his remarkable development, and that the Appendix, also chronological in arrangement, may serve those who wish for more.

The Poems

Seaside

Swiftly out from the friendly lilt of the band,
   The crowd's good laughter, the loved eyes of men,
   I am drawn nightward; I must turn again
Where, down beyond the low untrodden strand,
There curves and glimmers outward to the unknown
   The old unquiet ocean. All the shade
Is rife with magic and movement. I stray alone
   Here on the edge of silence, half afraid,

Waiting a sign. In the deep heart of me
The sullen waters swell towards the moon,
And all my tides set seaward.
               From inland
Leaps a gay fragment of some mocking tune,
That tinkles and laughs and fades along the sand,
And dies between the seawall and the sea.

1908

Failure

Because God put His adamantine fate
    Between my sullen heart and its desire,
I swore that I would burst the Iron Gate,
    Rise up, and curse Him on His throne of fire.
Earth shuddered at my crown of blasphemy,
    But Love was as a flame about my feet;
    Proud up the Golden Stair I strode; and beat
Thrice on the Gate, and entered with a cry –

All the great courts were quiet in the sun,
    And full of vacant echoes: moss had grown
Over the glassy pavement, and begun
    To creep within the dusty council-halls.
An idle wind blew round an empty throne
    And stirred the heavy curtains on the walls.

1908

The Jolly Company

The stars, a jolly company,
    I envied, straying late and lonely;
And cried upon their revelry:
    'O white companionship! You only
In love, in faith unbroken dwell,
Friends radiant and inseparable!'

Light-heart and glad they seemed to me
    And merry comrades (*even so*
God out of Heaven may laugh to see
    The happy crowds; and never know
That in his lone obscure distress
Each walketh in a wilderness).

But I, remembering, pitied well
    And loved them, who, with lonely light,
In empty infinite space dwell,
    Disconsolate. For all the night,
I heard the thin gnat-voices cry,
Star to faint star, across the sky.

November 1908

43

Epilogue in Heaven
from Life and Death of John Rump

. . . It may have become apparent that personally I do not approve of John Rump. He was a failure. He might have been a thousand splendid things. He was – an English Gentleman. He might have seen – he was blind; have heard – he was deaf. Infinite chances lay about him – he was an English Gentleman.

Yet we may pity him now, lying there through that long March night, helpless in the hands of his like. In that stuffy room were no watching angels, no 'Justice and Mercy of God', no 'Death as an Emperor with all his Court'. No sublimity or solemnity of leaving this world was there; no awe and pomp of dying; but worry, heat and tangled bed-clothes; an incompetent doctor, and tired-eyed, gulping relations; injections of oxygen and God knows what; and, bared of gentility, John Rump, blue-lipped, fighting for breath, helpless and pitiable as a blind kitten in a water-butt, or an insect crushed underfoot; drugs and fuss, gasping and snivelling.

Outside, in the snow-covered town, perfectly silent under the faint approach of morning, were peace and mystery, colour and beauty and joy; things that John had never known.

Epilogue in Heaven

(Everywhere there is a subdued air of expectancy. The archangels, massed effectively at the back, are wearing scarlet for the occasion. The harps and trumpets tune up. St. Cecilia waves the bâton. The first semi-chorus of angels on the left sings:)

Home out of time and space,
　　The wanderer is turning
　　　　Immortal feet;
The white and eager face,
　　The thirsting mouth and burning
　　　　Eyes we'll regreet, –
One that has found his grace,
　　One that has seaked his yearning,
　　　　One out of imperfection grown complete.

(Second semi-chorus on the right)

What will he bear with him, what will he bring to us
　　From the world where laughter and love are rife,
Great dreams to report to us, songs to sing to us,
　　Spoils well won from the heart of the strife?
Will he come like a glad-eyed silent lover,
　　Or slow and sorry that all is over,
Or sudden and splendid and swift as the spring to us,
　　Fresh and laughing from lovely life?

(Full chorus)

As the ending to a story,
　　As the light dies in the West
　　　　When the birds turn home at even,
　　　　　　Glad and splendid will he come,
He the victor into glory,
　　He the weary to his rest,
　　　　The immortal to his heaven,
　　　　　　The wanderer home.

FIRST SERAPH (*pointing downwards*) I see a speck immediately below.

MANY LITTLE CHERUBS Bravo! Bravo! Bravo!

SECOND SERAPH I see it too. A black speck. Very far!

CHERUBS Huzza! Huzza! Huzza!

THIRD SERAPH (*excitedly*) 'Tis him! 'Tis him! upon his upward way!

CHERUBS Hurray! Hurray! Hurray!

GOD (*rising*)

I do espy him like a *fretful midge*,
The while his wide and alternating vans
Winnow the buxom air. With flight serene
He wings amidst the watery Pleiades;
Now Leo feels his passage, and the Twins;
Orion now, and that unwieldy girth
Hight Scorpio; as when a trader bound
For Lamda or the isle of Mogador,
Freighted with ambergris and stilbrium,
And what rich odours . . .

(The remaining 127 lines are lost in the increasing hubbub.
Enter, from below on the left, JOHN RUMP in top-hat, frockcoat
etc., bearing an umbrella. He stands impassive in the middle.)

GOD

John Rump, of Balham, Leeds, and Canterbury,
Why are you wearing hideous black clothes?

RUMP

Because I am an English Gentleman.

GOD

John Rump, we gave you life and all its wonder.
What splendid tidings have you got to tell?

RUMP

God, I have been an English Gentleman.

GOD

Infinite splendour has been in your power;
John Rump, what have you got to show for life?

RUMP

God, I have been an English Gentleman.

GOD (*rising angrily*)

Was it for this we sent you to the world,
And gave you life and knowledge, made you man,
Crowned you with glory? You could have worked and laughed,

46

Sung, loved, and kissed, made all the world a dream,
Found infinite beauty in a leaf or word . . .
. . . Perish eternally, you and your hat!

RUMP (*not wincing*)

You long haired aesthetes, get you out of heaven!
I, John Rump, I, an English Gentleman,
Do not believe in you and all your gushing.
I am John Rump, this is my hat, and this
My umberella. I stand here for sense,
Invincible, inviolable, eternal,
For safety, regulations, paving-stones,
Street lamps, police, and bijou-residences
Semi-detached. I stand for sanity,
Comfort, content, prosperity, top-hats,
Alcohol, collars, meat. Tariff Reform
Means higher wages and more work for all.

(As he speaks, GOD and the seraphic multitude grow faint, mistier and mistier, become ineffectually waving shadows, and vanish. The floor of Heaven rocks . . . the thrones and the glassy sea . . . all has vanished. JOHN RUMP remains, still and expressionless, leaning on his umbrella, growing larger and larger, infinitely menacing, filling the universe, blotting out the stars . . .)

Sonnet

Oh! Death will find me, long before I tire
  Of watching you; and swing me suddenly
Into the shade and loneliness and mire
  Of the last land! There, waiting patiently,

One day, I think, I'll feel a cool wind blowing,
  See a slow light across the Stygian tide,
And hear the Dead about me stir, unknowing,
  And tremble. And *I* shall know that you have died,

And watch you, a broad-browed and smiling dream,
  Pass, light as ever, through the lightless host,
Quietly ponder, start, and sway, and gleam –
  Most individual and bewildering ghost! –

And turn, and toss your brown delightful head
Amusedly, among the ancient Dead.

April 1909

Menelaus and Helen

I

Hot through Troy's ruin Menelaus broke
   To Priam's palace, sword in hand, to sate
   On that adulterous whore a ten years' hate
And a king's honour. Through red death, and smoke,
And cries, and then by quieter ways he strode,
   Till the still innermost chamber fronted him.
   He swung his sword, and crashed into the dim
Luxurious bower, flaming like a god.

High sat white Helen, lonely and serene.
   He had not remembered that she was so fair,
And that her neck curved down in such a way;
And he felt tired. He flung the sword away,
   And kissed her feet, and knelt before her there,
The perfect Knight before the perfect Queen.

II

So far the poet. How should he behold
   That journey home, the long connubial years?
   He does not tell you how white Helen bears
Child on legitimate child, becomes a scold,
Haggard with virtue. Menelaus bold
   Waxed garrulous, and sacked a hundred Troys
   'Twixt noon and supper. And her golden voice
Got shrill as he grew deafer. And both were old.

Often he wonders why on earth he went
   Troyward, or why poor Paris ever came.
Oft she weeps, gummy-eyed and impotent;

Her dry shanks twitch at Paris' mumbled name.
So Menelaus nagged; and Helen cried;
And Paris slept on by Scamander side.

1909

Day and Night

Through my heart's palace Thoughts unnumbered
    throng;
  And there, most quiet and, as a child, most wise,
High-throned you sit, and gracious. All day long
  Great Hopes gold-armoured, jester Fantasies,
  And pilgrim Dreams, and little beggar Sighs,
Bow to your benediction, go their way.
  And the grave jewelled courtier Memories
Worship and love and tend you, all the day.

But, when I sleep, and all my thoughts go straying,
  When the high session of the day is ended,
And darkness comes; then, with the waning light,
  By lilied maidens on your way attended,
Proud from the wonted throne, superbly swaying,
  You, like a queen, pass out into the night.

1909

Victory

All night the ways of Heaven were desolate,
   Long roads across a gleaming empty sky.
   Outcast and doomed and driven, you and I,
Alone, serene beyond all love or hate,
Terror or triumph, were content to wait,
   We, silent and all-knowing. Suddenly
   Swept through the heaven, low-crouching from on high,
One horseman, downward to the earth's low gate.

Oh, perfect from the ultimate height of living,
   Lightly we turned, through wet woods blossom-hung,
Into the open. Down the supernal roads,
   With plumes a-tossing, purple flags far-flung,
Rank upon rank, unbridled, unforgiving,
   Thundered the black battalions of the Gods.

June 1909

A Channel Passage

The damned ship lurched and slithered. Quiet and quick
   My cold gorge rose; the long sea rolled; I knew
I must think hard of something, or be sick;
   And could think hard of only one thing – *you*!
You, you alone could hold my fancy ever!
   And with you memories come, sharp pain, and dole.
Now there's a choice – heartache or tortured liver!
   A sea-sick body, or a you-sick soul!

Do I forget you? Retchings twist and tie me,
   Old meat, good meals, brown gobbets, up I throw.
Do I remember? Acrid return and slimy,
   The sobs and slobber of a last year's woe.
And still the sick ship rolls. 'Tis hard, I tell ye,
To choose 'twixt love and nausea, heart and belly.

December 1909

Dining-Room Tea

When you were there, and you, and you,
Happiness crowned the night; I too,
Laughing and looking, one of all,
I watched the quivering lamplight fall
On plate and flowers and pouring tea
And cup and cloth; and they and we
Flung all the dancing moments by
With jest and glitter. Lip and eye
Flashed on the glory, shone and cried,
Improvident, unmemoried;
And fitfully and like a flame
The light of laughter went and came.
Proud in their careless transience moved
The changing faces that I loved.

Till suddenly, and otherwhence,
I looked upon your innocence.
For lifted clear and still and strange
From the dark woven flow of change
Under a vast and starless sky
I saw the immortal moment lie.
One instant I, an instant, knew
As God knows all. And it and you
I, above Time, oh, blind! could see
In witless immortality.
I saw the marble cup; the tea,
Hung on the air, an amber stream;
I saw the fire's unglittering gleam,
The painted flame, the frozen smoke.
No more the flooding lamplight broke
On flying eyes and lips and hair;

But lay, but slept unbroken there,
On stiller flesh, and body breathless,
And lips and laughter stayed and deathless,
And words on which no silence grew.
Light was more alive than you.
For suddenly, and otherwhence,
I looked on your magnificence.
I saw the stillness and the light,
And you, august, immortal, white,
Holy and strange; and every glint
Posture and jest and thought and tint
Freed from the mask of transiency,
Triumphant in eternity,
Immote, immortal.

                   Dazed at length
Human eyes grew, mortal strength
Wearied; and Time began to creep.
Change closed about me like a sleep.
Light glinted on the eyes I loved.
The cup was filled. The bodies moved.
The drifting petal came to ground.
The laughter chimed its perfect round.
The broken syllable was ended.
And I, so certain and so friended,
How could I cloud, or how distress,
The heaven of your unconsciousness?
Or shake at Time's sufficient spell,
Stammering of lights unutterable?
The eternal holiness of you,
The timeless end, you never knew,
The peace that lay, the light that shone.
You never knew that I had gone
A million miles away, and stayed
A million years. The laughter played
Unbroken round me; and the jest
Flashed on. And we that knew the best
Down wonderful hours grew happier yet.

I sang at heart, and talked, and ate,
And lived from laugh to laugh, I too,
When you were there, and you, and you.

c. 1910

Kindliness

When love has changed to kindliness –
Oh, love, our hungry lips, that press
So tight that Time's an old god's dream
Nodding in heaven, and whisper stuff
Seven million years were not enough
To think on after, make it seem
Less than the breath of children playing,
A blasphemy scarce worth the saying,
A sorry jest, 'When love has grown
To kindliness – to kindliness!' . . .
And yet – the best that either's known
Will change, and wither, and be less,
At last, than comfort, or its own
Remembrance. And when some caress
Tendered in habit (once a flame
All heaven sang out to) wakes the shame
Unworded, in the steady eyes
We'll have, – *that* day, what shall we do?
Being so noble, kill the two
Who've reached their second-best? Being wise,
Break cleanly off, and get away,
Follow down other windier skies
New lures, alone? Or shall we stay,
Since this is all we've known, content
In the lean twilight of such day,
And not remember, not lament?
That time when all is over, and
Hand never flinches, brushing hand;
And blood lies quiet, for all you're near;
And it's but spoken words we hear,
Where trumpets sang; when the mere skies

Are stranger and nobler than your eyes;
And flesh is flesh, was flame before;
And infinite hungers leap no more
In the chance swaying of your dress;
And love has changed to kindliness.

Sonnet

I said I splendidly loved you; it's not true.
    Such long swift tides stir not a land-locked sea.
On gods or fools the high risk falls – on you –
    The clean clear bitter-sweet that's not for me.
Love soars from earth to ecstasies unwist.
    Love is flung Lucifer-like from Heaven to Hell.
But – there are wanderers in the middle mist,
    Who cry for shadows, clutch, and cannot tell
Whether they love at all, or, loving, whom:
    An old song's lady, a fool in fancy dress,
Or phantoms, or their own face on the gloom;
    For love of Love, or from heart's loneliness.
Pleasure's not theirs, nor pain. They doubt, and sigh
    And do not love at all. Of these am I.

January 1910

Success

I think if you had loved me when I wanted;
   If I'd looked up one day, and seen your eyes,
And found my wild sick blasphemous prayer granted,
   And your brown face, that's full of pity and wise,
Flushed suddenly; the white godhead in new fear
   Intolerably so struggling, and so shamed;
Most holy and far, if you'd come all too near,
   If earth had seen Earth's lordliest wild limbs tamed,
Shaken, and trapped, and shivering, for *my* touch –
   Myself should I have slain? or that foul you?
But this the strange gods, who had given so much
   To have seen and known you, this they might not do.
One last shame's spared me, one black word's unspoken;
And I'm alone; and you have not awoken.

January 1910

Dust

When the white flame in us is gone,
    And we that lost the world's delight
Stiffen in darkness, left alone
    To crumble in our separate night;

When your swift hair is quiet in death,
    And through the lips corruption thrust
Has stilled the labour of my breath –
    When we are dust, when we are dust! –

Not dead, not undesirous yet,
    Still sentient, still unsatisfied,
We'll ride the air, and shine, and flit,
    Around the places where we died,

And dance as dust before the sun,
    And light of foot, and unconfined,
Hurry from road to road, and run
    About the errands of the wind.

And every mote, on earth or air,
    Will speed and gleam, down later days,
And like a secret pilgrim fare
    By eager and invisible ways,

Nor ever rest, nor ever lie,
    Till, beyond thinking, out of view,
One mote of all the dust that's I
    Shall meet one atom that was you.

Then in some garden hushed from wind,
    Warm in a sunset's afterglow,
The lovers in the flowers will find
    A sweet and strange unquiet grow

Upon the peace; and, past desiring,
    So high a beauty in the air,
And such a light, and such a quiring,
    And such a radiant ecstasy there,

They'll know not if it's fire, or dew,
    Or out of earth, or in the height,
Singing, or flame, or scent, or hue,
    Or two that pass, in light, to light,

Out of the garden higher, higher. . . .
    But in that instant they shall learn
The shattering ecstasy of our fire,
    And the weak passionless hearts will burn

And faint in that amazing glow,
    Until the darkness close above;
And they will know – poor fools, they'll know! –
    One moment, what it is to love.

December 1909–March 1910

The Life Beyond

He wakes, who never thought to wake again,
    Who held the end was Death. He opens eyes
Slowly, to one long livid oozing plain
    Closed down by the strange eyeless heavens. He lies;
    And waits; and once in timeless sick surmise
Through the dead air heaves up an unknown hand,
Like a dry branch. No life is in that land,
    Himself not lives, but is a thing that cries;
An unmeaning point upon the mud; a speck
    Of moveless horror; an Immortal One
Cleansed of the world, sentient and dead; a fly
    Fast-stuck in grey sweat on a corpse's neck.

I thought when love for you died, I should die.
It's dead. Alone, most strangely, I live on.

April – September 1910

Lines Written in the Belief that the Ancient Roman Festival of the Dead was called Ambarvalia

Swings the way still by hollow and hill,
    And all the world's a song;
'She's far,' it sings me, 'but fair,' it rings me,
    'Quiet,' it laughs, 'and strong!'

Oh! spite of the miles and years between us,
    Spite of your chosen part,
I do remember; and I go
    With laughter in my heart.

So above the little folk that know not,
    Out of the white hill-town,
High up I clamber; and I remember;
    And watch the day go down.

Gold is my heart, and the world's golden,
    And one peak tipped with light;
And the air lies still about the hill
    With the first fear of night;

Till mystery down the soundless valley
    Thunders, and dark is here;
And the wind blows, and the light goes,
    And the night is full of fear.

And I know, one night, on some far height,
    In the tongue I never knew,
I yet shall hear the tidings clear
    From them that were friends of you.

They'll call the news from hill to hill,
   Dark and uncomforted,
Earth and sky and the winds; and I
   Shall know that you are dead.

I shall not hear your trentals,
   Nor eat your arval bread;
For the kin of you will surely do
   Their duty by the dead.

Their little dull greasy eyes will water;
   They'll paw you, and gulp afresh.
They'll sniffle and weep, and their thoughts will creep
   Like flies on the cold flesh.

They will put pence on your grey eyes,
   Bind up your fallen chin,
And lay you straight, the fools that loved you
   Because they were your kin.

They will praise all the bad about you,
   And hush the good away,
And wonder how they'll do without you,
   And then they'll go away.

But quieter than one sleeping,
   And stranger than of old,
You will not stir for weeping,
   You will not mind the cold;

But through the night the lips will laugh not,
   The hands will be in place,
And at length the hair be lying still
   About the quiet face.

With snuffle and sniff and handkerchief,
   And dim and decorous mirth,
With ham and sherry, they'll meet to bury
   The lordliest lass of earth.

The little dead hearts will tramp ungrieving
    Behind lone-riding you,
The heart so high, the heart so living,
    Heart that they never knew.

I shall not hear your trentals,
    Nor eat your arval bread,
Nor with smug breath tell lies of death
    To the unanswering dead.

With snuffle and sniff and handkerchief,
    The folk who loved you not
Will bury you, and go wondering
    Back home. And you will rot.

But laughing and half-way up to heaven,
    With wind and hill and star,
I yet shall keep, before I sleep,
    Your Ambarvalia.

1910

The Hill

Breathless, we flung us on the windy hill,
   Laughed in the sun, and kissed the lovely grass.
   You said, 'Through glory and ecstasy we pass;
Wind, sun, and earth remain, the birds sing still,
When we are old, are old. . . .' 'And when we die
   All's over that is ours; and life burns on
Through other lovers, other lips,' said I,
   'Heart of my heart, our heaven is now, is won!'

'We are Earth's best, that learnt her lesson here.
   Life is our cry. We have kept the faith!' we said;
   'We shall go down with unreluctant tread
Rose-crowned into the darkness!' . . . Proud we were,
And laughed, that had such brave true things to say.
 – And then you suddenly cried, and turned away.

December 1910

Sonnet Reversed

Hand trembling towards hand; the amazing lights
Of heart and eye. They stood on supreme heights.

Ah, the delirious weeks of honeymoon!
    Soon they returned, and, after strange adventures,
Settled at Balham by the end of June.
    Their money was in Can. Pacs. B. Debentures,
And in Antofagastas. Still he went
    Cityward daily; still she did abide
At home. And both were really quite content
    With work and social pleasures. Then they died.
They left three children (besides George, who drank):
    The eldest Jane, who married Mr. Bell,
William, the head-clerk in the County Bank,
    And Henry, a stock-broker, doing well.

Lulworth, 1st January 1911

A Letter to a Live Poet

Sir, since the last Elizabethan died,
Or, rather, that more Paradisal muse,
Blind with much light, passed to the light more
   glorious
Or deeper blindness, no man's hand, as thine,
Has, on the world's most noblest chord of song,
Struck certain magic strains. Ears satiate
With the clamorous, timorous whisperings of to-day,
Thrilled to perceive once more the spacious voice
And serene utterance of old. We heard
  – With rapturous breath half-held, as a dreamer
   dreams
Who dares not know it dreaming, lest he wake –
The odorous, amorous style of poetry,
The melancholy knocking of those lines,
The long, low soughing of pentameters,
  – Or the sharp of rhyme as a bird's cry –
And the innumerable truant polysyllables
Multitudinously twittering like a bee.
Fulfilled our hearts were with that music then,
And all the evenings sighed it to the dawn,
And all the lovers heard it from all the trees.
All of the accents upon all the norms!
  – And ah! the stress on the penultimate!
We never knew blank verse could have such feet.

Where is it now? Oh, more than ever, now
I sometimes think no poetry is read
Save where some sepultured Cæsura bled,
Royally incarnadining all the line.
Is the imperial iamb laid to rest,

And the young trochee, having done enough?
Ah! turn again! Sing so to us, who are sick
Of seeming-simple rhymes, bizarre emotions,
Decked in the simple verses of the day,
Infinite meaning in a little gloom,
Irregular thoughts in stanzas regular,
Modern despair in antique metres, myths
Incomprehensible at evening,
And symbols that mean nothing in the dawn.
The slow lines swell. The new style sighs. The Celt
Moans round with many voices.
                      God! to see
Gaunt anapæsts stand up out of the verse,
Combative accents, stress where no stress should be,
Spondee on spondee, iamb on choriamb,
The thrill of all the tribrachs in the world,
And all the vowels rising to the E!
To hear the blessed mutter of those verbs,
Conjunctions passionate toward each other's arms,
And epithets like amaranthine lovers
Stretching luxuriously to the stars,
All prouder pronouns than the dawn, and all
The thunder of the trumpets of the noun!

January 1911

Thoughts on the Shape of the Human Body

How can we find? how can we rest? how can
We, being gods, win joy, or peace, being man?
We, the gaunt zanies of a witless Fate,
Who love the unloving, and the lover hate,
Forget the moment ere the moment slips,
Kiss with blind lips that seek beyond the lips,
Who want, and know not what we want, and cry
With crooked mouths for Heaven, and throw it by.
Love's for completeness! No perfection grows
'Twixt leg, and arm, elbow, and ear, and nose,
And joint, and socket; but unsatisfied
Sprawling desires, shapeless, perverse, denied.
Finger with finger wreathes; we love, and gape,
Fantastic shape to mazed fantastic shape,
Straggling, irregular, perplexed, embossed,
Grotesquely twined, extravagantly lost
By crescive paths and strange protuberant ways
From sanity and from wholeness and from grace.
How can love triumph, how can solace be,
Where fever turns toward fever, knee toward knee?
Could we but fill to harmony, and dwell
Simple as our thought and as perfectible,
Rise disentangled from humanity
Strange whole and new into simplicity,
Grow to a radiant round love, and bear
Unfluctuant passion for some perfect sphere,
Love moon to moon unquestioning, and be
Like the star Lunisequa, steadfastly
Following the round clear orb of her delight,
·Patiently ever, through the eternal night!

c. 1911

Dead Men's Love

There was a damned successful Poet;
　　There was a Woman like the Sun.
And they were dead. They did not know it.
　　They did not know their time was done.
　　　　They did not know his hymns
　　　　Were silence; and her limbs,
　　　　That had served Love so well,
　　　　Dust, and a filthy smell.

And so one day, as ever of old,
　　Hands out, they hurried, knee to knee;
On fire to cling and kiss and hold
　　And, in the other's eyes, to see
　　　　Each his own tiny face,
　　　　And in that long embrace
　　　　Feel lip and breast grow warm
　　　　To breast and lip and arm.

So knee to knee they sped again,
　　And laugh to laugh they ran, I'm told,
Across the streets of Hell . . .
　　　　　　　　　　And then
　　They suddenly felt the wind blow cold,
　　　　And knew, so closely pressed,
　　　　Chill air on lip and breast,
　　　　And, with a sick surprise,
　　　　The emptiness of eyes.

Munich, 27th February 1911

72

Colloquial

It was not that you said I thought you knew,
Or that you thought I said that you, my dear,
Felt what I felt you felt. If it were clear,
Had God given soul to me, or sense to you,
Or guts, indeed, to either of the two,
Had it been worth a smile, or worth a tear,
Heart of my heart.

February 1911

Mummia

As those of old drank mummia
   To fire their limbs of lead,
Making dead kings from Africa
   Stand pander to their bed;

Drunk on the dead, and medicined
   With spiced imperial dust,
In a short night they reeled to find
   Ten centuries of lust.

So I, from paint, stone, tale, and rhyme,
   Stuffed love's infinity,
And sucked all lovers of all time
   To rarefy ecstasy.

Helen's the hair shuts out from me
   Verona's livid skies;
Gypsy the lips I press; and see
   Two Antonys in your eyes.

The unheard invisible lovely dead
   Lie with us in this place,
And ghostly hands above my head
   Close face to straining face;

Their blood is wine along our limbs;
   Their whispering voices wreathe
Savage forgotten drowsy hymns
   Under the names we breathe;

Woven from their tomb, and one with it,
  The night wherein we press;
Their thousand pitchy pyres have lit
  Your flaming nakedness.

For the uttermost years have cried and clung
  To kiss your mouth to mine;
And hair long dust was caught, was flung,
  Hand shaken to hand divine,

And Life has fired, and Death not shaded,
  All Time's uncounted bliss,
And the height o' the world has flamed and faded, –
  Love, that our love be this!

1911

The Fish

In a cool curving world he lies
And ripples with dark ecstasies.
The kind luxurious lapse and steal
Shapes all his universe to feel
And know and be; the clinging stream
Closes his memory, glooms his dream,
Who lips the roots o' the shore, and glides
Superb on unreturning tides.
Those silent waters weave for him
A fluctuant mutable world and dim,
Where wavering masses bulge and gape
Mysterious, and shape to shape
Dies momently through whorl and hollow,
And form and line and solid follow
Solid and line and form to dream
Fantastic down the eternal stream;
An obscure world, a shifting world,
Bulbous, or pulled to thin, or curled,
Or serpentine, or driving arrows,
Or serene slidings, or March narrows.
There slipping wave and shore are one,
And weed and mud. No ray of sun,
But glow to glow fades down the deep
(As dream to unknown dream in sleep);
Shaken translucency illumes
The hyaline of drifting glooms;
The strange soft-handed depth subdues
Drowned colour there, but black to hues,
As death to living, decomposes –
Red darkness of the heart of roses,
Blue brilliant from dead starless skies,

And gold that lies behind the eyes,
The unknown unnameable sightless white
That is the essential flame of night,
Lustreless purple, hooded green,
The myriad hues that lie between
Darkness and darkness! . . .

                              And all's one
Gentle, embracing, quiet, dun,
The world he rests in, world he knows,
Perpetual curving. Only – grows
An eddy in that ordered falling,
A knowledge from the gloom, a calling
Weed in the wave, gleam in the mud –
The dark fire leaps along his blood;
Dateless and deathless, blind and still,
The intricate impulse works its will;
His woven world drops back; and he,
Sans providence, sans memory,
Unconscious and directly driven,
Fades to some dank sufficient heaven.

O world of lips, O world of laughter,
Where hope is fleet and thought flies after,
Of lights in the clear night, of cries
That drift along the wave and rise
Thin to the glittering stars above,
You know the hands, the eyes of love!
The strife of limbs, the sightless clinging
The infinite distance, and the singing
Blown by the wind, a flame of sound,
The gleam, the flowers, and vast around
The horizon, and the heights above –
You know the sigh, the song of love!

But there the night is close, and there
Darkness is cold and strange and bare;
And the secret deeps are whisperless;

And rhythm is all deliciousness;
And joy is in the throbbing tide,
Whose intricate fingers beat and glide
In felt bewildering harmonies
Of trembling touch; and music is
The exquisite knocking of the blood.
Space is no more, under the mud;
His bliss is older than the sun.
Silent and straight the waters run.
The lights, the cries, the willows dim,
And the dark tide are one with him.

Munich, March 1911

Sometimes Even Now . . .

Sometimes even now I may
Steal a prisoner's holiday,
Slip, when all is worst, the bands,
   Hurry back, and duck beneath
Time's old tyrannous groping hands,
   Speed away with laughing breath
Back to all I'll never know,
Back to you, a year ago.

Truant there from Time and Pain,
What I had, I find again:
Sunlight in the boughs above,
   Sunlight in your hair and dress,
The Hands too proud for all but Love,
   The Lips of utter kindliness,
The Heart of bravery swift and clean
   Where the best was safe, I knew,
And laughter in the gold and green,
   And song, and friends, and ever you
With smiling and familiar eyes,
   You – but friendly: you – but true.

And Innocence accounted wise,
   And Faith the fool, the pitiable.
Love so rare, one would swear
   All of earth for ever well –
Careless lips and flying hair,
   And little things I may not tell.

It does but double the heart-ache
When I wake, when I wake.

c. 1912

79

Fragment on Painters

There is an evil which that Race attaints
Who represent God's World with oily paints,
Who mock the Universe, so rare and sweet,
With spots of colour on a canvas sheet,
Defile the Lovely and insult the Good
By scrawling upon little bits of wood.
They'd snare the moon, and catch the immortal sun
With madder brown and pale vermilion,
Entrap an English evening's magic hush . . .

c. 1912

In Freiburg Station

In Freiburg station, waiting for a train,
I saw a Bishop in puce gloves go by.
Now God may thunder furious from the sky,
Shattering all my glory into pain,
And joy turn stinking rotten, hope be vain,
Night fall on little laughters, little loves,
And better Bishops don more glorious gloves,
While I go down in darkness; what care I?

There is one memory God can never break,
There is one splendour more than all the pain,
There is one secret that shall never die,
Star-crowned I stand and sing, for that hour's sake.
In Freiburg station, waiting for a train,
I saw a Bishop with puce gloves go by.

1912

Travel

'Twas when I was in Neu Strelitz
I broke my heart in little bits.

So while I sat in the Müritz train
I glued the bits together again.

But when I got to Amerhold,
I felt the glue would never hold.

And now that I'm home to Barton Hill,
I know once broken is broken still.

1912

The Old Vicarage, Grantchester

(Café des Westens, Berlin, May 1912)

Just now the lilac is in bloom,
All before my little room;
And in my flower-beds, I think,
Smile the carnation and the pink;
And down the borders, well I know,
The poppy and the pansy blow . . .
Oh! there the chestnuts, summer through,
Beside the river make for you
A tunnel of green gloom, and sleep
Deeply above; and green and deep
The stream mysterious glides beneath,
Green as a dream and deep as death.
 – Oh, damn! I know it! and I know
How the May fields all golden show,
And when the day is young and sweet,
Gild gloriously the bare feet
That run to bathe . . .
                    Du lieber Gott!

Here am I, sweating, sick, and hot,
And there the shadowed waters fresh
Lean up to embrace the naked flesh.
Temperamentvoll German Jews
Drink beer around; – and *there* the dews
Are soft beneath a morn of gold.
Here tulips bloom as they are told;
Unkempt about those hedges blows
An English unofficial rose;
And there the unregulated sun
Slopes down to rest when day is done,

And wakes a vague unpunctual star,
A slippered Hesper; and there are
Meads towards Haslingfield and Coton
Where *das Betreten*'s not *verboten*.

εἴθε γενοίμην . . . would I were
In Grantchester, in Grantchester! –
Some, it may be, can get in touch
With Nature there, or Earth, or such.
And clever modern men have seen
A Faun a-peeping through the green,
And felt the Classics were not dead,
To glimpse a Naiad's reedy head,
Or hear the Goat-foot piping low: . . .
But these are things I do not know.
I only know that you may lie
Day-long and watch the Cambridge sky,
And, flower-lulled in sleepy grass,
Hear the cool lapse of hours pass,
Until the centuries blend and blur
In Grantchester, in Grantchester. . . .
Still in the dawnlit waters cool
His ghostly Lordship swims his pool,
And tries the strokes, essays the tricks,
Long learnt on Hellespont, or Styx.
Dan Chaucer hears his river still
Chatter beneath a phantom mill.
Tennyson notes, with studious eye,
How Cambridge waters hurry by . . .
And in that garden, black and white,
Creep whispers through the grass all night;
And spectral dance, before the dawn,
A hundred Vicars down the lawn;
Curates, long dust, will come and go
On lissom, clerical, printless toe;
And oft between the boughs is seen
The sly shade of a Rural Dean . . .
Till, at a shiver in the skies,

Vanishing with Satanic cries,
The prim ecclesiastic rout
Leaves but a startled sleeper-out,
Grey heavens, the first bird's drowsy calls,
The falling house that never falls.

God! I will pack, and take a train,
And get me to England once again!
For England's the one land, I know,
Where men with Splendid Hearts may go;
And Cambridgeshire, of all England,
The shire for Men who Understand;
And of *that* district I prefer
The lovely hamlet Grantchester.
For Cambridge people rarely smile,
Being urban, squat, and packed with guile;
And Royston men in the far South
Are black and fierce and strange of mouth;
At Over they fling oaths at one,
And worse than oaths at Trumpington,
And Ditton girls are mean and dirty,
And there's none in Harston under thirty,
And folks in Shelford and those parts
Have twisted lips and twisted hearts,
And Barton men make Cockney rhymes,
And Coton's full of nameless crimes,
And things are done you'd not believe
At Madingley, on Christmas Eve.
Strong men have run for miles and miles,
When one from Cherry Hinton smiles;
Strong men have blanched, and shot their wives,
Rather than send them to St. Ives;
Strong men have cried like babes, bydam,
To hear what happened at Babraham.
But Grantchester! ah, Grantchester!
There's peace and holy quiet there,
Great clouds along pacific skies,
And men and women with straight eyes,

Lithe children lovelier than a dream,
A bosky wood, a slumbrous stream,
And little kindly winds that creep
Round twilight corners, half asleep.
In Grantchester their skins are white;
They bathe by day, they bathe by night;
The women there do all they ought;
The men observe the Rules of Thought.
They love the Good; they worship Truth;
They laugh uproariously in youth;
(And when they get to feeling old,
They up and shoot themselves, I'm told) . . .
Ah God! to see the branches stir
Across the moon at Grantchester!
To smell the thrilling-sweet and rotten
Unforgettable, unforgotten
River-smell, and hear the breeze
Sobbing in the little trees.
Say, do the elm-clumps greatly stand
Still guardians of that holy land?
The chestnuts shade, in reverend dream,
The yet unacademic stream?
Is dawn a secret shy and cold
Anadyomene, silver-gold?
And sunset still a golden sea
From Haslingfield to Madingley?
And after, ere the night is born,
Do hares come out about the corn?
Oh, is the water sweet and cool,
Gentle and brown, above the pool?
And laughs the immortal river still
Under the mill, under the mill?
Say, is there Beauty yet to find?
And Certainty? and Quiet kind?
Deep meadows yet, for to forget
The lies, and truths, and pain? . . . Oh! yet
Stands the Church clock at ten to three?
And is there honey still for tea?

Beauty and Beauty

When Beauty and Beauty meet
   All naked, fair to fair,
The earth is crying-sweet,
   And scattering-bright the air,
Eddying, dizzying, closing round,
   With soft and drunken laughter;
Veiling all that may befall
   After – after –

Where Beauty and Beauty met,
   Earth's still a-tremble there,
And the winds are scented yet,
   And memory-soft the air,
Bosoming, folding glints of light,
   And shreds of shadowy laughter;
Not the tears that fill the years
   After – after –

1912

Song

All suddenly the wind comes soft,
   And Spring is here again;
And the hawthorn quickens with buds of green,
   And my heart with buds of pain.

My heart all Winter lay so numb,
   The earth so dead and frore,
That I never thought the Spring would come,
   Or my heart wake any more.

But Winter's broken and earth has woken,
   And the small birds cry again;
And the hawthorn hedge puts forth its buds,
   And my heart puts forth its pain.

1912

Mary and Gabriel

Young Mary, loitering once her garden way,
Felt a warm splendour grow in the April day,
As wine that blushes water through. And soon,
Out of the gold air of the afternoon,
One knelt before her: hair he had, or fire,
Bound back above his ears with golden wire,
Baring the eager marble of his face.
Not man's nor woman's was the immortal grace
Rounding the limbs beneath that robe of white,
And lighting the proud eyes with changeless light,
Incurious. Calm as his wings, and fair,
That presence filled the garden.
                                    She stood there,
Saying, 'What would you, Sir?'
                                    He told his word,
'Blessed art thou of women!' Half she heard,
Hands folded and face bowed, half long had known,
The message of that clear and holy tone,
That fluttered hot sweet sobs about her heart;
Such serene tidings moved such human smart.
Her breath came quick as little flakes of snow.
Her hands crept up her breast. She did but know
It was not hers. She felt a trembling stir
Within her body, a will too strong for her
That held and filled and mastered all. With eyes
Closed, and a thousand soft short broken sighs,
She gave submission; fearful, meek, and glad. . . .
   She wished to speak. Under her breasts she had
Such multitudinous burnings, to and fro,
And throbs not understood; she did not know
If they were hurt or joy for her; but only
That she was grown strange to herself, half lonely,

All wonderful, filled full of pains to come
And thoughts she dare not think, swift thoughts and dumb,
Human, and quaint, her own, yet very far,
Divine, dear, terrible, familiar . . .
Her heart was faint for telling; to relate
Her limbs' sweet treachery, her strange high estate,
Over and over, whispering, half revealing,
Weeping; and so find kindness to her healing.
'Twixt tears and laughter, panic hurrying her,
She raised her eyes to that fair messenger.
He knelt unmoved, immortal; with his eyes
Gazing beyond her, calm to the calm skies;
Radiant, untroubled in his wisdom, kind.
His sheaf of lilies stirred not in the wind.
How should she, pitiful with mortality,
Try the wide peace of that felicity
With ripples of her perplexed shaken heart,
And hints of human ecstasy, human smart,
And whispers of the lonely weight she bore,
And how her womb within was hers no more
And at length hers?
     Being tired, she bowed her head;
And said, 'So be it!'
       The great wings were spread,
Showering glory on the fields, and fire.
The whole air, singing, bore him up, and higher,
Unswerving, unreluctant. Soon he shone
A gold speck in the gold skies; then was gone.

The air was colder, and grey. She stood alone.

Autumn 1912

90

Unfortunate

Heart, you are restless as a paper scrap
  That's tossed down dusty pavements by the wind;
  Saying, 'She is most wise, patient and kind.
Between the small hands folded in her lap
Surely a shamed head may bow down at length,
  And find forgiveness where the shadows stir
About her lips, and wisdom in her strength,
  Peace in her peace. Come to her, come to her!' . . .

She will not care. She'll smile to see me come,
  So that I think all Heaven in flower to fold me.
  She'll give me all I ask, kiss me and hold me,
    And open wide upon that holy air
The gates of peace, and take my tiredness home,
    Kinder than God. But, heart, she will not care.

1912

The True Beatitude

(BOUTS-RIMÉS)

They say, when the Great Prompter's hand shall ring
  Down the last curtain upon earth and sea,
  All the Good Mimes will have eternity
To praise their Author, worship love and sing;
Or to the walls of Heaven wandering
  Look down on those damned for a fretful d – ,
  Mock them (all theologians agree
On this reward for virtue), laugh, and fling

New sulphur on the sin-incarnadined . . .
  Ah, Love! still temporal, and still atmospheric,
    Teleologically unperturbed,
We share a peace by no divine divined,
  An earthly garden hidden from any cleric,
    Untrodden of God, by no Eternal curbed.

1913

Song

The way of Love was thus.
He was born, one winter morn,
With hands delicious.
And it was well with us.

Love came our quiet way,
Lit pride in us, and died in us,
All in a winter's day.
There is no more to say.

1913

The Busy Heart

Now that we've done our best and worst, and parted,
    I would fill my mind with thoughts that will not rend.
(O heart, I do not dare go empty-hearted)
    I'll think of Love in books, Love without end;
Women with child, content; and old men sleeping;
    And wet strong ploughlands, scarred for certain grain;
And babes that weep, and so forget their weeping;
    And the young heavens, forgetful after rain;
And evening hush, broken by homing wings;
    And Song's nobility, and Wisdom holy,
That live, we dead. I would think of a thousand things,
    Lovely and durable, and taste them slowly,
One after one, like tasting a sweet food.
I have need to busy my heart with quietude.

1913

The Young Man in April

In the queer light, in twilight,
    In April of the year,
I meet a thousand women,
    But I never meet my Dear.
Yet each of them has something,
    A turn of neck or knee,
A line of breast or shoulder,
    That brings my Dear to me.

One has a way of swaying,
    I'd swear to anywhere;
One has a laugh, and one a hat,
    And one a trick of hair;
 – Oh, glints and hints and gestures,
    When shall I find complete
The Dear that's walking somewhere,
    The Dear I've yet to meet?

May 1913

It's not going to Happen Again

I have known the most dear that is granted us here,
    More supreme than the gods know above,
Like a star I was hurled through the sweet of the world,
    And the height and the light of it, Love.
I have risen to the uttermost Heaven of Joy,
    I have sunk to the sheer Hell of Pain –
But – it's not going to happen again, my boy,
    It's not going to happen again.

It's the very first word that poor Juliet heard
    From her Romeo over the Styx;
And the Roman will tell Cleopatra in hell
    When she starts the immortal old tricks;
What Paris was tellin' for good-bye to Helen
    When he bundled her into the train –
Oh, it's not going to happen again, old girl,
    It's not going to happen again.

Château Lake Louise
Canada 1913

Love

Love is a breach in the walls, a broken gate,
    Where that comes in that shall not go again;
Love sells the proud heart's citadel to Fate.
    They have known shame, who love unloved. Even then
When two mouths, thirsty each for each, find slaking,
    And agony's forgot, and hushed the crying
Of credulous hearts, in heaven – such are but taking
    Their own poor dreams within their arms, and lying
Each in his lonely night, each with a ghost.
    Some share that night. But they know, love grows colder,
Grows false and dull, that was sweet lies at most.
    Astonishment is no more in hand or shoulder,
But darkens, and dies out from kiss to kiss.
All this is love; and all love is but this.

1913

The Chilterns

Your hands, my dear, adorable,
  Your lips of tenderness
– Oh, I've loved you faithfully and well,
  Three years, or a bit less.
  It wasn't a success.

Thank God, that's done! and I'll take the road,
  Quit of my youth and you,
The Roman road to Wendover
  By Tring and Lilley Hoo,
  As a free man may do.

For youth goes over, the joys that fly,
  The tears that follow fast;
And the dirtiest things we do must lie
  Forgotten at the last;
  Even Love goes past.

What's left behind I shall not find,
  The splendour and the pain;
The splash of sun, the shouting wind,
  And the brave sting of rain,
  I may not meet again.

But the years, that take the best away,
  Give something in the end;
And a better friend than love have they,
  For none to mar or mend,
  That have themselves to friend.

I shall desire and I shall find
   The best of my desires;
The autumn road, the mellow wind
   That soothes the darkening shires,
   And laughter, and inn-fires.

White mist about the black hedgerows,
   The slumbering Midland plain,
The silence where the clover grows,
   And the dead leaves in the lane,
   Certainly, these remain.

And I shall find some girl perhaps,
   And a better one than you,
With eyes as wise, but kindlier,
   And lips as soft, but true.
   And I daresay she will do.

1913

Home

I came back late and tired last night
   Into my little room,
To the long chair and the firelight
   And comfortable gloom.

But as I entered softly in
   I saw a woman there,
The line of neck and cheek and chin,
   The darkness of her hair,
The form of one I did not know
   Sitting in my chair.

I stood a moment fierce and still,
   Watching her neck and hair.
I made a step to her; and saw
   That there was no one there.

It was some trick of the firelight
   That made me see her there.
It was a chance of shade and light
   And the cushion in the chair.

Oh, all you happy over the earth,
   That night, how could I sleep?
I lay and watched the lonely gloom;
   And watched the moonlight creep
From wall to basin, round the room.
   All night I could not sleep.

1913

The Night Journey

Hands and lit faces eddy to a line;
   The dazed last minutes click; the clamour dies.
Beyond the great-swung arc o' the roof, divine,
   Night, smoky-scarv'd, with thousand coloured eyes

Glares the imperious mystery of the way.
   Thirsty for dark, you feel the long-limbed train
Throb, stretch, thrill motion, slide, pull out and sway,
   Strain for the far, pause, draw to strength again. . . .

 – As a man, caught by some great hour, will rise,
   Slow-limbed, to meet the light or find his love;
And, breathing long, with staring sightless eyes,
   Hands out, head back, agape and silent, move

Sure as a flood, smooth as a vast wind blowing;
   And, gathering power and godhead as he goes,
Unstumbling, unreluctant, strong, unknowing,
   Borne by a will not his, that lifts, that grows,

Sweep into darkness, triumphing to his goal,
   Out of the fire, out of the little room! . . .
 – There is an end appointed, O my soul!
   Crimson and green the signals burn. The gloom

Is hung with steam's fantastic livid streamers.
   Lost into God, as lights in light, we fly,
Grown one with will, end-drunken huddled dreamers.
   The white lights roar; the sounds of the world die;

And lips and laughter are forgotten things.
    Speed sharpens; grows. Into the night, and on,
The strength and splendour of our purpose swings.
    The lamps fade; and the stars. We are alone.

1913

The Way that Lovers Use

The way that lovers use is this;
   They bow, catch hands, with never a word,
And their lips meet, and they do kiss,
   – So I have heard.

They queerly find some healing so,
   And strange attainment in the touch;
There is a secret lovers know,
   – I have read as much.

And theirs no longer joy nor smart,
   Changing or ending, night or day;
But mouth to mouth, and heart on heart,
   – So lovers say.

1913

The Funeral of Youth: Threnody

The day that *Youth* had died,
There came to his grave-side,
In decent mourning, from the country's ends,
Those scatter'd friends
Who had lived the boon companions of his prime,
And laughed with him and sung with him and wasted,
In feast and wine and many-crown'd carouse,
The days and nights and dawnings of the time
When *Youth* kept open house,
Nor left untasted
Aught of his high emprise and ventures dear,
No quest of his unshar'd –
All these, with loitering feet and sad head bar'd,
Followed their old friend's bier.
Folly went first,
With muffled bells and coxcomb still revers'd;
And after trod the bearers, hat in hand –
Laughter, most hoarse, and Captain *Pride* with tanned
And martial face all grim, and fussy *Joy*,
Who had to catch a train, and *Lust*, poor snivelling boy;
These bore the dear departed.
Behind them, broken-hearted,
Came *Grief*, so noisy a widow, that all said,
'Had he but wed
Her elder sister *Sorrow*, in her stead!'
And by her, trying to soothe her all the time,
The fatherless children, *Colour, Tune*, and *Rhyme*,
(The sweet lad *Rhyme*), ran all-uncomprehending.
Then, at the way's sad ending,
Round the raw grave they stay'd. Old *Wisdom* read
In mumbling tone the Service for the Dead.

There stood *Romance*,
The furrowing tears had mark'd her rougèd cheek;
Poor old *Conceit*, his wonder unassuag'd;
Dead *Innocency's* daughter, *Ignorance*;
And shabby, ill-dress'd *Generosity*;
And *Argument*, too full of woe to speak;
Passion, grown portly, something middle-ag'd;
And *Friendship* – not a minute older, she;
Impatience, ever taking out his watch;
Faith, who was deaf, and had to lean, to catch
Old *Wisdom's* endless drone.
Beauty was there,
Pale in her black; dry-eyed; she stood alone.
Poor maz'd *Imagination; Fancy* wild;
Ardour, the sunlight on his greying hair;
Contentment, who had known *Youth* as a child
And never seen him since. And *Spring* came too,
Dancing over the tombs, and brought him flowers –
She did not stay for long.
And *Truth*, and *Grace*, and all the merry crew,
The laughing *Winds* and *Rivers*, and lithe *Hours*;
And *Hope*, the dewy-eyed; and sorrowing *Song*; –
Yes, with much woe and mourning general,
At dead *Youth's* funeral,
Even these were met once more together, all,
Who erst the fair and living *Youth* did know;
All, except only *Love*. *Love* had died long ago.

1913

Mutability

They say there's a high windless world and strange,
   Out of the wash of days and temporal tide,
   Where Faith and Good, Wisdom and Truth abide,
Æterna corpora, subject to no change.

There the sure suns of these pale shadows move;
   There stand the immortal ensigns of our war;
   Our melting flesh fixed Beauty there, a star,
And perishing hearts, imperishable Love. . . .

Dear, we know only that we sigh, kiss, smile;
   Each kiss lasts but the kissing; and grief goes over;
   Love has no habitation but the heart.
Poor straws! on the dark flood we catch awhile,
   Cling, and are borne into the night apart.
   The laugh dies with the lips, 'Love' with the lover.

South Kensington — Makaweli, 1913

He wonders whether to Praise or to Blame Her

I have peace to weigh your worth, now all is over,
    But if to praise or blame you, cannot say.
For, who decries the loved, decries the lover;
    Yet what man lauds the thing he's thrown away?

Be you, in truth, this dull, slight, cloudy naught,
    The more fool I, so great a fool to adore;
But if you're that high goddess once I thought,
    The more your godhead is, I lose the more.

Dear fool, pity the fool who thought you clever!
    Dear wisdom, do not mock the fool that missed you!
Most fair, – the blind has lost your face for ever!
    Most foul, – how could I see you while I kissed you?

So . . . the poor love of fools and blind I've proved you,
For, foul or lovely, 'twas a fool that loved you.

1913

Doubts

When she sleeps, her soul, I know,
Goes a wanderer on the air,
Wings where I may never go,
Leaves her lying, still and fair,
Waiting, empty, laid aside,
Like a dress upon a chair. . . .
This I know, and yet I know
Doubts that will not be denied.

For if the soul be not in place,
What has laid trouble in her face?
And, sits there nothing ware and wise
Behind the curtains of her eyes,
What is it, in the self's eclipse,
Shadows, soft and passingly,
About the corners of her lips,
The smile that is essential she?

And if the spirit be not there,
Why is fragrance in the hair?

1913

There's Wisdom in Women

'Oh love is fair, and love is rare;' my dear one she said,
'But love goes lightly over.' I bowed her foolish head,
And kissed her hair and laughed at her. Such a child was she;
So new to love, so true to love, and she spoke so bitterly.

But there's wisdom in women, of more than they have known,
And thoughts go blowing through them, are wiser than their
    own,
Or how should my dear one, being ignorant and young,
Have cried on love so bitterly, with so true a tongue?

June 1913

Clouds

Down the blue night the unending columns press
   In noiseless tumult, break and wave and flow,
   Now tread the far South, or lift rounds of snow
Up to the white moon's hidden loveliness.
Some pause in their grave wandering comradeless,
   And turn with profound gesture vague and slow,
   As who would pray good for the world, but know
Their benediction empty as they bless.

They say that the Dead die not, but remain
   Near to the rich heirs of their grief and mirth.
     I think they ride the calm mid-heaven, as these,
In wise majestic melancholy train,
    And watch the moon, and the still-raging seas,
   And men, coming and going on the earth.

The Pacific, October 1913

Sonnet

*(Suggested by some of the Proceedings of the Society for
Psychical Research)*

Not with vain tears, when we're beyond the sun,
   We'll beat on the substantial doors, nor tread
   Those dusty high-roads of the aimless dead
Plaintive for Earth; but rather turn and run
Down some close-covered by-way of the air,
   Some low sweet alley between wind and wind,
   Stoop under faint gleams, thread the shadows, find
Some whispering ghost-forgotten nook, and there
Spend in pure converse our eternal day;
   Think each in each, immediately wise;
Learn all we lacked before; hear, know, and say
   What this tumultuous body now denies;
And feel, who have laid our groping hands away;
   And see, no longer blinded by our eyes.

1913

A Memory

(From a sonnet-sequence)

Somewhile before the dawn I rose, and stept
   Softly along the dim way to your room,
   And found you sleeping in the quiet gloom,
And holiness about you as you slept.
I knelt there; till your waking fingers crept
   About my head, and held it. I had rest
   Unhoped this side of Heaven, beneath your breast.
I knelt a long time, still; nor even wept.

It was great wrong you did me; and for gain
Of that poor moment's kindliness, and ease,
And sleepy mother-comfort!
                 Child, you know
How easily love leaps out to dreams like these,
Who has seen them true. And love that's wakened so
Takes all too long to lay asleep again.

Waikiki, October 1913

112

One Day

To-day I have been happy. All the day
   I held the memory of you, and wove
Its laughter with the dancing light o' the spray,
   And sowed the sky with tiny clouds of love,
And sent you following the white waves of sea,
   And crowned your head with fancies, nothing worth,
Stray buds from that old dust of misery,
   Being glad with a new foolish quiet mirth.

So lightly I played with those dark memories,
Just as a child, beneath the summer skies,
   Plays hour by hour with a strange shining stone,
For which (he knows not) towns were fire of old,
   And love has been betrayed, and murder done,
And great kings turned to a little bitter mould.

The Pacific, October 1913

Waikiki

Warm perfumes like a breath from vine and tree
    Drift down the darkness. Plangent, hidden from eyes,
    Somewhere an *eukaleli* thrills and cries
And stabs with pain the night's brown savagery;
And dark scents whisper; and dim waves creep to me,
    Gleam like a woman's hair, stretch out, and rise;
    And new stars burn into the ancient skies,
Over the murmurous soft Hawaian sea.

And I recall, lose, grasp, forget again,
    And still remember, a tale I have heard, or known,
An empty tale, of idleness and pain,
    Of two that loved – or did not love – and one
Whose perplexed heart did evil, foolishly,
A long while since, and by some other sea.

Waikiki, 1913

Heaven

Fish (fly-replete, in depth of June,
Dawdling away their wat'ry noon)
Ponder deep wisdom, dark or clear,
Each secret fishy hope or fear.
Fish say, they have their Stream and Pond;
But is there anything Beyond?
This life cannot be All, they swear,
For how unpleasant, if it were!
One may not doubt that, somehow, Good
Shall come of Water and of Mud;
And, sure, the reverent eye must see
A Purpose in Liquidity.
We darkly know, by Faith we cry,
The future is not Wholly Dry.
Mud unto mud! – Death eddies near –
Not here the appointed End, not here!
But somewhere, beyond Space and Time,
Is wetter water, slimier slime!
And there (they trust) there swimmeth One
Who swam ere rivers were begun,
Immense, of fishy form and mind,
Squamous, omnipotent, and kind;
And under that Almighty Fin,
The littlest fish may enter in.
Oh! never fly conceals a hook,
Fish say, in the Eternal Brook,
But more than mundane weeds are there,
And mud, celestially fair;
Fat caterpillars drift around,
And Paradisal grubs are found;
Unfading moths, immortal flies,

And the worm that never dies.
And in that Heaven of all their wish,
There shall be no more land, say fish.

1913

Fragment (from a geometrical 'Heaven')

Eternal Rhombus strong to save

The Oval is a deathless Oval there
And the Great Square eternally a Square.

And One who says ''Ere Euclid was, I AM,''
The sempiternal Parallelogram.

            The Eternal Curve
Jostled for ever by the Eternal Line

Fafaïa

Stars that seem so close and bright,
Watched by lovers through the night,
Swim in emptiness, men say,
Many a mile and year away.

And yonder star that burns so white,
May have died to dust and night
Ten, maybe, or fifteen year,
Before it shines upon my dear.

Oh! often among men below,
Heart cries out to heart, I know,
And one is dust a many years,
Child, before the other hears.

Heart from heart is all as far,
Fafaïa, as star from star.

Saanapu, November 1913

118

Hauntings

In the grey tumult of these after-years
   Oft silence falls; the incessant wranglers part;
And less-than-echoes of remembered tears
   Hush all the loud confusion of the heart;
And a shade, through the toss'd ranks of mirth and crying,
   Hungers, and pains, and each dull passionate mood, –
Quite lost, and all but all forgot, undying,
   Comes back the ecstasy of your quietude.

So a poor ghost, beside his misty streams,
Is haunted by strange doubts, evasive dreams,
   Hints of a pre-Lethean life, of men,
Stars, rocks, and flesh, things unintelligible,
   And light on waving grass, he knows not when,
And feet that ran, but where, he cannot tell.

The Pacific, 1914

119

The Great Lover

I have been so great a lover: filled my days
So proudly with the splendour of Love's praise,
The pain, the calm, and the astonishment,
Desire illimitable, and still content,
And all dear names men use, to cheat despair,
For the perplexed and viewless streams that bear
Our hearts at random down the dark of life.
Now, ere the unthinking silence on that strife
Steals down, I would cheat drowsy Death so far,
My night shall be remembered for a star
That outshone all the suns of all men's days.
Shall I not crown them with immortal praise
Whom I have loved, who have given me, dared with me
High secrets, and in darkness knelt to see
The inenarrable godhead of delight?
Love is a flame: – we have beaconed the world's night.
A city: – and we have built it, these and I.
An emperor: – we have taught the world to die.
So, for their sakes I loved, ere I go hence,
And the high cause of Love's magnificence,
And to keep loyalties young, I'll write those names
Golden for ever, eagles, crying flames,
And set them as a banner, that men may know,
To dare the generations, burn, and blow
Out on the wind of Time, shining and streaming. . . .
These I have loved:

          White plates and cups, clean-gleaming,
Ringed with blue lines; and feathery, faery dust;
Wet roofs, beneath the lamp-light; the strong crust
Of friendly bread; and many-tasting food;
Rainbows; and the blue bitter smoke of wood;

And radiant raindrops couching in cool flowers;
And flowers themselves, that sway through sunny hours,
Dreaming of moths that drink them under the moon;
Then, the cool kindliness of sheets, that soon
Smooth away trouble; and the rough male kiss
Of blankets; grainy wood; live hair that is
Shining and free; blue-massing clouds; the keen
Unpassioned beauty of a great machine;
The benison of hot water; furs to touch;
The good smell of old clothes; and others such –
The comfortable smell of friendly fingers,
Hair's fragrance, and the musty reek that lingers
About dead leaves and last year's ferns. . . .

       Dear names,
And thousand other throng to me! Royal flames;
Sweet water's dimpling laugh from tap or spring;
Holes in the ground; and voices that do sing;
Voices in laughter, too; and body's pain,
Soon turned to peace; and the deep-panting train;
Firm sands; the little dulling edge of foam
That browns and dwindles as the wave goes home;
And washen stones, gay for an hour; the cold
Graveness of iron; moist black earthen mould;
Sleep; and high places; footprints in the dew;
And oaks; and brown horse-chestnuts, glossy-new;
And new-peeled sticks; and shining pools on grass; –
All these have been my loves. And these shall pass,
Whatever passes not, in the great hour,
Nor all my passion, all my prayers, have power
To hold them with me through the gate of Death.
They'll play deserter, turn with the traitor breath,
Break the high bond we made, and sell Love's trust
And sacramented covenant to the dust.
——Oh, never a doubt but, somewhere, I shall wake,
And give what's left of love again, and make
New friends, now strangers. . . .

      But the best I've known
Stays here, and changes, breaks, grows old, is blown

About the winds of the world, and fades from brains
Of living men, and dies.
                              Nothing remains.

O dear my loves, O faithless, once again
This one last gift I give: that after men
Shall know, and later lovers, far-removed,
Praise you, 'All these were lovely'; say, 'He loved.'

Mataiea, 1914

Retrospect

In your arms was still delight,
Quiet as a street at night;
And thoughts of you, I do remember,
Were green leaves in a darkened chamber,
Were dark clouds in a moonless sky.
Love, in you, went passing by,
Penetrative, remote, and rare,
Like a bird in the wide air,
And, as the bird, it left no trace
In the heaven of your face.

In your stupidity I found
The sweet hush after a sweet sound.
All about you was the light
That dims the greying end of night;
Desire was the unrisen sun,
Joy the day not yet begun,
With tree whispering to tree,
Without wind, quietly.
Wisdom slept within your hair,
And Long-Suffering was there,
And, in the flowing of your dress,
Undiscerning Tenderness.
And when you thought, it seemed to me,
Infinitely, and like a sea,
About the slight world you had known
Your vast unconsciousness was thrown. . . .
O haven without wave or tide!
Silence, in which all songs have died!
Holy book, where hearts are still!
And home at length under the hill!

O mother-quiet, breasts of peace,
Where love itself would faint and cease!
O infinite deep I never knew,
I would come back, come back to you,
Find you, as a pool unstirred,
Kneel down by you, and never a word,
Lay my head, and nothing said,
In your hands, ungarlanded;
And a long watch you would keep;
And I should sleep, and I should sleep!

Mataiea, January 1914

Tiare Tahiti

Mamua, when our laughter ends,
And hearts and bodies, brown as white,
Are dust about the doors of friends,
Or scent a-blowing down the night,
Then, oh! then, the wise agree,
Comes our immortality.
Mamua, there waits a land
Hard for us to understand.
Out of time, beyond the sun,
All are one in Paradise,
You and Pupure* are one,
And Taü, and the ungainly wise.
There the Eternals are, and there
The Good, the Lovely, and the True,
And Types, whose earthly copies were
The foolish broken things we knew;
There is the Face, whose ghosts we are;
The real, the never-setting Star;
And the Flower, of which we love
Faint and fading shadows here;
Never a tear, but only Grief;
Dance, but not the limbs that move;
Songs in Song shall disappear;
Instead of lovers, Love shall be;
For hearts, Immutability;
And there, on the Ideal Reef,
Thunders the Everlasting Sea!

And my laughter, and my pain,
Shall home to the Eternal Brain.
And all lovely things, they say,

*Tahitian for 'fair', the name given to himself.

Meet in Loveliness again;
Miri's laugh, Teïpo's feet,
And the hands of Matua,
Stars and sunlight there shall meet,
Coral's hues and rainbows there,
And Teüra's braided hair;
And with the starred *tiare's* white,
And white birds in the dark ravine,
And *flamboyants* ablaze at night,
And jewels, and evening's after-green,
And dawns of pearl and gold and red,
Mamua, your lovelier head!
And there'll no more be one who dreams
Under the ferns, of crumbling stuff,
Eyes of illusion, mouth that seems,
All time-entangled human love.
And you'll no longer swing and sway
Divinely down the scented shade,
Where feet to Ambulation fade,
And noons are lost in endless Day.
How shall we wind these wreaths of ours,
Where there are neither heads nor flowers?
Oh, Heaven's Heaven! – but we'll be missing
The palms, and sunlight, and the south;
And there's an end, I think, of kissing,
When our mouths are one with Mouth . . .

Taü here, Mamua,
Crown the hair, and come away!
Here the calling of the moon,
And the whispering scents that stray
About the idle warm lagoon.
Hasten, hand in human hand,
Down the dark, the flowered way,
Along the whiteness of the sand,
And in the water's soft caress,
Wash the mind of foolishness,
Mamua, until the day.

Spend the glittering moonlight there
Pursuing down the soundless deep
Limbs that gleam and shadowy hair,
Or floating lazy, half-asleep.
Dive and double and follow after,
Snare in flowers, and kiss, and call,
With lips that fade, and human laughter,
And faces individual,
Well this side of Paradise! . . .
There's little comfort in the wise.

Papeete, February 1914

The Treasure

When colour goes home into the eyes,
   And lights that shine are shut again,
With dancing girls and sweet birds' cries
   Behind the gateways of the brain;
And that no-place which gave them birth, shall close
The rainbow and the rose: –

Still may Time hold some golden space
   Where I'll unpack that scented store
Of song and flower and sky and face,
   And count, and touch, and turn them o'er,
Musing upon them; as a mother, who
Has watched her children all the rich day through,
Sits, quiet-handed, in the fading light,
When children sleep, ere night.

August 1914

1914

I. Peace

Now, God be thanked Who has matched us with His hour,
  And caught our youth, and wakened us from sleeping,
With hand made sure, clear eye, and sharpened power,
  To turn, as swimmers into cleanness leaping,
Glad from a world grown old and cold and weary,
  Leave the sick hearts that honour could not move,
And half-men, and their dirty songs and dreary,
  And all the little emptiness of love!

Oh! we, who have known shame, we have found release there,
  Where there's no ill, no grief, but sleep has mending,
    Naught broken save this body, lost but breath;
Nothing to shake the laughing heart's long peace there
  But only agony, and that has ending;
    And the worst friend and enemy is but Death.

II. Safety

Dear! of all happy in the hour, most blest
   He who has found our hid security,
Assured in the dark tides of the world that rest,
   And heard our word, 'Who is so safe as we?'
We have found safety with all things undying,
   The winds, and morning, tears of men and mirth,
The deep night, and birds singing, and clouds flying,
   And sleep, and freedom, and the autumnal earth.

We have built a house that is not for Time's throwing.
   We have gained a peace unshaken by pain for ever.
War knows no power. Safe shall be my going,
   Secretly armed against all death's endeavour;
Safe though all safety's lost; safe where men fall;
And if these poor limbs die, safest of all.

III. The Dead

Blow out, you bugles, over the rich Dead!
   There's none of these so lonely and poor of old,
   But, dying, has made us rarer gifts than gold.
These laid the world away; poured out the red
Sweet wine of youth; gave up the years to be
   Of work and joy, and that unhoped serene,
   That men call age; and those who would have been,
Their sons, they gave, their immortality.

Blow, bugles, blow! They brought us, for our dearth,
   Holiness, lacked so long, and Love, and Pain.
Honour has come back, as a king, to earth,
   And paid his subjects with a royal wage;
And Nobleness walks in our ways again;
   And we have come into our heritage.

IV. The Dead

These hearts were woven of human joys and cares,
    Washed marvellously with sorrow, swift to mirth.
The years had given them kindness. Dawn was theirs,
    And sunset, and the colours of the earth.
These had seen movement, and heard music; known
    Slumber and waking; loved; gone proudly friended;
Felt the quick stir of wonder; sat alone;
    Touched flowers and furs and cheeks. All this is ended.

There are waters blown by changing winds to laughter
And lit by the rich skies, all day. And after,
    Frost, with a gesture, stays the waves that dance
And wandering loveliness. He leaves a white
    Unbroken glory, a gathered radiance,
A width, a shining peace, under the night.

V. The Soldier

If I should die, think only this of me:
   That there's some corner of a foreign field
That is for ever England. There shall be
   In that rich earth a richer dust concealed;
A dust whom England bore, shaped, made aware,
   Gave, once, her flowers to love, her ways to roam,
A body of England's, breathing English air,
   Washed by the rivers, blest by suns of home.

And think, this heart, all evil shed away,
   A pulse in the eternal mind, no less
     Gives somewhere back the thoughts by England given;
Her sights and sounds; dreams happy as her day;
   And laughter, learnt of friends; and gentleness,
     In hearts at peace, under an English heaven.

November–December 1914

The Dance

A SONG

As the Wind, and as the Wind,
   In a corner of the way,
Goes skipping, stands twirling,
Invisibly, comes whirling,
Bows before, and skips behind,
   In a grave, an endless play –

So my Heart, and so my Heart,
   Following where your feet have gone,
Stirs dust of old dreams there;
He turns a toe; he gleams there,
Treading you a dance apart.
   But you see not. You pass on.

April 1915

Fragments
written during the voyage to Gallipoli
April 1915

I strayed about the deck, an hour, to-night
Under a cloudy moonless sky; and peeped
In at the windows, watched my friends at table,
Or playing cards, or standing in the doorway,
Or coming out into the darkness. Still
No one could see me.

                 I would have thought of them
– Heedless, within a week of battle – in pity,
Pride in their strength and in the weight and firmness
And link'd beauty of bodies, and pity that
This gay machine of splendour'ld soon be broken,
Thought little of, pashed, scattered. . . .

                  Only, always,
I could but see them – against the lamplight – pass
Like coloured shadows, thinner than filmy glass,
Slight bubbles, fainter than the wave's faint light,
That broke to phosphorus out in the night,
Perishing things and strange ghosts – soon to die
To other ghosts – this one, or that, or I.

Lines for an Ode-Threnody on England

All things are written in the mind.
There the sure hills have station; and the wind
Blows   in that placeless air.
And there the white and golden birds go flying;
And the stars wheel and shine; and woods are fair;
The light upon the snow is there;
                              and in that nowhere move
The trees and hands and waters that we love.

And she for whom we die, she the undying
Mother of men
England!

In Avons of the heart her rivers run.

She is with all we have loved and found and known,
Closed in the little nowhere of the brain.
Only, of all our dreams,
Not the poor heap of . . . dust and stone,
This local earth, set in terrestrial streams,
Not this man, giving all for gold,
Nor that who has found evil good, nor these
Blind millions, bought and sold . . .

She is not here, or now –
She is here, and now, yet nowhere –
We gave her birth, who bore us –
Our wandering feet have sought, but never found her –
She is built a long way off –
She, though all men be traitors, not betrayed –
Whose soil is love, and her stars justice, she –

Gracious with flowers,
And robed . . . and glorious in the sea.*

She was in his eyes, but he could not see her,
And he was England, but he knew her not.

*E.M. notes: 'This last set of lines, or rather jottings, is not written as if they were meant to be consecutive.'

Fragment of a Sonnet

The poor scrap of a song that some man tried
Down in the troop-decks forrard, brought again
The day you sang it first, on a hill-side,
With April in the wind and in the brain.
And the woods were gold; and youth was in our hands.

                        Oh lovers parted,
Oh all you lonely over all the world,
You that look out at morning empty-hearted,
Or you, all night turning uncomforted.

Would God, would God, you could be comforted.

                        Eyes that weep,
And a long time for love, and, after, sleep.

Fragment of a poem about Evening

And daylight, like a dust, sinks through the air,
And drifting, golds the ground . . .
                                        A lark,
A voice in heaven, in fading deeps of light,
Drops, at length, home.
A wind of night, shy as the young hare
That steals even now out of the corn to play,
Stirs the pale river once, and creeps away.

Fragment of an Elegy

The feet that ran with mine have found their goal,
The eyes that met my eyes have looked on night.
The firm limbs are no more; gone back to earth.
Easily mingling . . .

What he is yet,

Not living, lives, hath place in a few minds . . .

He wears

The ungathered blossom of quiet; stiller he
Than a deep well at noon, or lovers met;
Than sleep, or the heart after wrath. He is
The silence following great words of peace.

Appendix to the Poems

A Sicilian Octave

An Evil Time came down with fateful feet
    And trod across the garden of my soul –
Before him grass and tender herbs were sweet,
    But still behind him desolation stole.
Stark thorns and thistle hedge a waste complete,
    Wide-spread beneath the adverse stars' control;
How shall the frail hands of my spirit meet
    The change – or make the marrèd beauty whole?

1905

Translation of Horace Liber I Carmen XXXVIII

Fellow, I hate your pomp of Paris,
Those neat green garlands you propose.
No longer seek the spot where tarries
The last red rose.

We only want some simple shrub
That will disgrace nor you, the stripling
Waiter, nor me in village pub
Placidly tippling.

c. 1906

Hymn 666 (The Stockbroker's Book of Hymns, Revised & Augmented)

Lord, on this calm and holy day,
We fall before thy shrine to pray,
Because we hope to make it pay,
   Giver of all.

No mystics we, plain businessmen;
We kneel, and rise, and kneel again:
It rather bores us, Lord – but then
   Thou givest all.

Whatever, Lord, we lend to thee,
Repaid a thousand-fold shall be;
Then gladly do we give to thee,
   Giver of all.

One hundred thousand, Lord, per cent,
Is useful gain on what we lent;
To thee all English knees are bent,
   Who givest all.

Commercial Christianity
Is now a paying company,
With a financial deity
   For capital:

Sixpence a week towards the poor
Will make the eternal millions sure;
O jewelled walls! O golden floor!
   O Lord of all.
                Amen

c. 1906

Under a picture of a schoolmaster

For Forty years he has taught Greek.
He gets about Four Pounds a Week.
He speaks in Patient Monotones.
His Name is Jones.

c. 1906

Ballade (To J.B.S[*trachey*].)

Boys! mine is not a pleasant task to-day;
But to the pure everything is pure.
(Levinstein do not fidget!) Let us Pray . . .
You often must have noticed, I am sure,
When washing in your little tub or ewer,
Or wondering How God fashioned you, or worse
Yielding to Curiosity's base lure, –
Between your legs there hangs a bag, or purse.

Sir! have you wondered why the world is grey?
Why I am grim and hollow-eyed, and you're
Snappy, and She is singing all the day?
(You often must have noticed, I am sure),
Some say, the higher that we go, the fewer.
Some, there's a purpose in the universe . . .
Look down, young man! The thing is not obscure,
Between your legs there hangs a bag, or purse.

This was suggested by a pamphlet issued by some agency for promoting purity among the young by informing them of physiological facts, which angered R.B. The 4th and 8th lines in each stanza are quotations from it.

c. 1906

The Song of the Beasts

(Sung, on one night, in the cities, in the darkness)

Come away! Come away!
Ye are sober and dull through the common day,
But now it is night!
It is shameful night, and God is asleep!
(Have you not felt the quick fires that creep
Through the hungry flesh, and the lust of delight,
And hot secrets of dreams that day cannot say?). . . .
. . . The house is dumb;
The night calls out to you. . . . Come, ah, come!
Down the dim stairs, through the creaking door,
Naked, crawling on hands and feet
 – It is meet! it is meet!
Ye are men no longer, but less and more,
Beast and God. . . . Down the lampless street,
By little black ways, and secret places,
In darkness and mire,
Faint laughter around, and evil faces
By the star-glint seen – ah! follow with us!
For the darkness whispers a blind desire,
And the fingers of night are amorous. . . .
Keep close as we speed,
Though mad whispers woo you, and hot hands cling,
And the touch and the smell of bare flesh sting,
Soft flank by your flank, and side brushing side –
Tonight never heed!
Unswerving and silent follow with me,
Till the city ends sheer,
And the crook'd lanes open wide,
Out of the voices of night,

148

Beyond lust and fear,
To the level waters of moonlight,
To the level waters, quiet and clear,
To the black unresting plains of the calling sea.

1906

The Vision of the Archangels

Slowly up silent peaks, the white edge of the world,
   Trod four archangels, clear against the unheeding sky,
Bearing, with quiet even steps, and great wings furled,
   A little dingy coffin; where a child must lie,
It was so tiny. (Yet, you had fancied, God could never
   Have bidden a child turn from the spring and the sunlight,
And shut him in that lonely shell, to drop for ever
   Into the emptiness and silence, into the night. . . .)

They then from the sheer summit cast, and watched it fall,
   Through unknown glooms, that frail black coffin –
     and therein
   God's little pitiful Body lying, worn and thin,
And curled up like some crumpled, lonely flower-petal –
Till it was no more visible; then turned again
With sorrowful quiet faces downward to the plain.

December 1906

The Beginning

Some day I shall rise and leave my friends
And seek you again through the world's far ends,
You whom I found so fair,
(Touch of your hands and smell of your hair!),
My only god in the days that were.
My eager feet shall find you again,
Though the sullen years and the mark of pain
Have changed you wholly; for I shall know
(How could I forget having loved you so?),
In the sad half-light of evening,
The face that was all my sunrising.
So then at the ends of the earth I'll stand
And hold you fiercely by either hand,
And seeing your age and ashen hair
I'll curse the thing that once you were,
Because it is changed and pale and old
(Lips that were scarlet, hair that was gold!),
And I loved you before you were old and wise,
When the flame of youth was strong in your eyes,
 – And my heart is sick with memories.

January 1907

The Call

Out of the nothingness of sleep,
   The slow dreams of Eternity,
There was a thunder on the deep:
   I came, because you called to me.

I broke the Night's primeval bars,
   I dared the old abysmal curse,
And flashed through ranks of frightened stars
   Suddenly on the universe!

The eternal silences were broken;
   Hell became Heaven as I passed. –
What shall I give you as a token,
   A sign that we have met, at last?

I'll break and forge the stars anew,
   Shatter the heavens with a song;
Immortal in my love for you,
   Because I love you, very strong.

Your mouth shall mock the old and wise,
   Your laugh shall fill the world with flame,
I'll write upon the shrinking skies
   The scarlet splendour of your name,

Till Heaven cracks, and Hell thereunder
   Dies in her ultimate mad fire,
And darkness falls, with scornful thunder,
   On dreams of men and men's desire.

Then only in the empty spaces,
   Death, walking very silently,
Shall fear the glory of our faces
   Through all the dark infinity.

So, clothed about with perfect love,
   The eternal end shall find us one,
Alone above the Night, above
   The dust of the dead gods, alone.

February 1907

From *Ballade of Middle Age*

[The young man]

He worships every foreign bore,
Ibsen and Nietzsche and Rousseau
And Dostoieffsky and Tagore
And (oh my God) D'Annunzio:
Each Scandinavian lust or woe,
Whose shallowness no plummet gauged,
Is his, for all his friends to know:
Thank God that we are middle-aged.

c. 1907

God's Song Book

(*Translation of 'Liederbuch der Gottheit' by Christian
Wagner*)

Glory of earth and sky and sea,
God's book of song He gives to me!
A child, I turn each page thereof,
And read, remembering His love.

Spring sunlight, upon fen and fold,
And every page is edged with gold!
Gay flowers between the leaves are pressed
To mark the songs we love the best.

1907

A Comment

God gives us, in earth's loveliness,
   His own great song-book, it is stated.
We stumble through, (and have to guess
   To whom or what it's dedicated!)

On first perusing, how we yearn to
   Mark every song! but soon, my friend,
The only page we want to turn to
   Holds two best words of all, 'The End'.

But, since we've got to read it through,
   Let us, as true philosophers,
Sit down, and critically review
   God's *very* minor book of verse.

One poem I've underlined – the best –
   (There's all sorts in God's poetry-book!):
But of the lot I most detest
   God's vulgar lyric 'Rupert Brooke'.

          . . .

And, if you're lenient, and declare
   The faults and merits pretty equal,
At least you'll join my hearty prayer
   'Dear Author, *please* don't write a sequel!'

1907

Song

Oh! that apple bloom, and the pale spring sun
And the cottage door;
I'll see them all, before I've done,
A many Aprils more.

And you, for all your fairy feet,
And your strange brown ways,
Won't wholly for ever by wood or street
Avoid one owlish gaze.

But – suddenly you, in white and blue,
By the cottage door,
And the blue and white of April weather,
And the apple-bloom – just these together
I'll see no more, no more.

c. 1907

Dawn

(From the train between Bologna and Milan, second class)

Opposite me two Germans snore and sweat.
   Through sullen swirling gloom we jolt and roar.
We have been here for ever: even yet
   A dim watch tells two hours, two aeons, more.
The windows are tight-shut and slimy-wet
   With a night's fœtor. There are two hours more;
Two hours to dawn and Milan; two hours yet.
   Opposite me two Germans sweat and snore. . . .

One of them wakes, and spits, and sleeps again.
   The darkness shivers. A wan light through the rain
Strikes on our faces, drawn and white. Somewhere
   A new day sprawls; and, inside, the foul air
Is chill, and damp, and fouler than before. . . .
   Opposite me two Germans sweat and snore.

1907

Ante Aram

Before thy shrine I kneel, an unknown worshipper,
   Chanting strange hymns to thee and sorrowful litanies,
Incense of dirges, prayers that are as holy myrrh.

Ah! goddess, on thy throne of tears and faint low sighs,
   Weary at last to theeward come the feet that err,
And empty hearts grown tired of the world's vanities.

How fair this cool deep silence to a wanderer
   Deaf with the roar of winds along the open skies!
Sweet, after sting and bitter kiss of sea-water,

The pale Lethean wine within thy chalices! . . .
   I come before thee, I, too tired wanderer
To heed the horror of the shrine, the distant cries,

And evil whispers in the gloom, or the swift whirr
   Of terrible wings – I, least of all thy votaries,
With a faint hope to see the scented darkness stir,

And, parting, frame within its quiet mysteries
   One face, with lips than autumn-lilies tenderer,
And voice more sweet than the far plaint of viols is,

   Or the soft moan of any grey-eyed lute-player.

June 1907

The Wayfarers

Is it the hour? We leave this resting-place
   Made fair by one another for a while.
Now, for a god-speed, one last mad embrace;
   The long road then, unlit by your faint smile.
Ah! the long road! and you so far away!
Oh, I'll remember! but . . . each crawling day
   Will pale a little your scarlet lips, each mile
Dull the dear pain of your remembered face.

. . . Do you think there's a far border town,
     somewhere,
   The desert's edge, last of the lands we know,
   Some gaunt eventual limit of our light,
  In which I'll find you waiting; and we'll go
Together, hand in hand again, out there,
    Into the waste we know not, into the night?

June 1907

The Little Dog's Day

All in the town were still asleep,
When the sun came up with a shout and a leap.
In the lonely streets unseen by man,
A little dog danced. And the day began.

All his life he'd been good, as far as he could,
And the poor little beast had done all that he should.
But this morning he swore, by Odin and Thor
And the Canine Valhalla – he'd stand it no more!
So his prayer he got granted – to do just what he wanted,
Prevented by none, for the space of one day.
'Jam incipiebo,[1] *sedere facebo,'*[2]
In dog-Latin he quoth, *'Euge! sophos! hurray!'*

He fought with the he-dogs, and winked at the she-dogs,
A thing that had never been *heard* of before.
'For the stigma of gluttony, I care not a button!' he
Cried, and ate all he could swallow – and more.

He took sinewy lumps from the shins of old frumps,
And mangled the errand-boys – when he could get 'em.
He shammed furious *rabies,*[3] and bit all the babies,[3]
And followed the cats up the trees, and then ate 'em!

They thought 'twas the devil was holding a revel,
And sent for the parson to drive him away;
For the town never knew such a hullaballoo
As that little dog raised – till the end of that day.

When the blood-red sun had gone burning down,
And the lights were lit in the little town,

Outside, in the gloom of the twilight grey,
The little dog died when he'd had his day. *

July 1907

[1]Now we're off.
[2]*I'll* make them sit up.
[3]Pronounce either to suit rhyme.

*This last stanza, by another hand, was set as the 'problem' for competitors in the Saturday *Westminster Gazette*, July 1907.

Song of the Children in Heaven

In evil places far away
And naughty times for ever gone
We were so good, the Angels say,
That now God lets us sit upon
The golden floor of glassy stone.

He is so good and kind, and yet
(Don't tell Him) the great floor of glass
Is rather hard. We can't forget
The bad old world. We wish it was
Just warm, sweet-smelling, tumbly grass.

And when on whistles and toy drums
We make a loud amusing noise,
Some large official seraph comes
And scolds, and takes away our toys,
Bids us sit still and be good boys.

And when a baby laughs up here
Or rolls his crown about in play,
There is a pause. God looks severe;
The Angels frown, and sigh and pray,
And some-one takes the crown away.

August 1907

Sonnet: in time of Revolt

The thing must End. I am no boy! I AM
  NO BOY!! being twenty-one. Uncle, you make
  A great mistake, a very great mistake,
In chiding me for letting slip a 'Damn!'
What's more, you called me 'Mother's one ewe lamb,'
  Bade me 'refrain from swearing – for *her* sake –
  Till I'm grown up' . . . – By God! I think you take
Too much upon you, Uncle William!

You say I am your brother's only son.
I know it. And, 'What of it?' I reply.
My heart's resolvéd. *Something must be done.*
So shall I curb, so baffle, so suppress
This too avuncular officiousness,
Intolerable consanguinity.

January 1908

In Examination

Lo! from quiet skies
In through the window my Lord the Sun!
And my eyes
Were dazzled and drunk with the misty gold,
The golden glory that drowned and crowned me
Eddied and swayed through the room . . .

                             Around me,
To left and to right,
Hunched figures and old,
Dull blear-eyed scribbling fools, grew fair,
Ringed round and haloed with holy light.
Flame lit on their hair,
And their burning eyes grew young and wise,
Each as a God, or King of kings,
White-robed and bright
(Still scribbling all);
And a full tumultuous murmur of wings
Grew through the hall;
And I knew the white undying Fire,
And, through open portals,
Gyre on gyre,
Archangels and angels, adoring, bowing,
And a Face unshaded. . . .
Till the light faded;
And they were but fools again, fools unknowing,
Still scribbling, blear-eyed and stolid immortals.

February 1908

Wagner

Creeps in half wanton, half asleep,
   One with a fat wide hairless face.
He likes love-music that is cheap;
   Likes women in a crowded place;
      And wants to hear the noise they're making.

His heavy eyelids droop half-over,
   Great pouches swing beneath his eyes.
He listens, thinks himself the lover,
   Heaves from his stomach wheezy sighs;
      He likes to feel his heart's a-breaking.

The music swells. His gross legs quiver.
   His little lips are bright with slime.
The music swells. The women shiver.
   And all the while, in perfect time,
      His pendulous stomach hangs a-shaking.

Queen's Hall, 1908

On the Death of Smet-Smet, the Hippopotamus Goddess

SONG OF A TRIBE OF THE ANCIENT EGYPTIANS

(*The Priests within the Temple*)
She was wrinkled and huge and hideous? She was our Mother.
She was lustful and lewd? – but a God; we had none other.
In the day She was hidden and dumb, but at nightfall moaned in
　　the shade;
We shuddered and gave Her Her will in the darkness;
　　we were afraid.

(*The People without*)
　　　　　She sent us pain,
　　　　　　And we bowed before Her;
　　　　　She smiled again
　　　　　　And bade us adore Her.
　　　　　She solaced our woe
　　　　　　And soothed our sighing;
　　　　　And what shall we do
　　　　　　Now God is dying?

(*The Priests within*)
She was hungry and ate our children; – how should we stay Her?
She took our young men and our maidens; – ours to obey Her.
We were loathèd and mocked and reviled of all nations; that
　　was our pride.
She fed us, protected us, loved us, and killed us; now She has
　　died.

167

(The People without)

> She was so strong;
>   But Death is stronger.
> She ruled us long;
>   But Time is longer.
> She solaced our woe
>   And soothed our sighing;
> And what shall we do
>   Now God is dying?

1908

The Song of the Pilgrims

(Halted around the fire by night, after moon-set, they sing this beneath the trees)

What light of unremembered skies
Hast thou relumed within our eyes,
Thou whom we seek, whom we shall find? . . .
A certain odour on the wind,
Thy hidden face beyond the west,
These things have called us; on a quest
Older than any road we trod,
More endless than desire. . . .

                                      Far God,
Sigh with thy cruel voice, that fills
The soul with longing for dim hills
And faint horizons! For there come
Grey moments of the antient dumb
Sickness of travel, when no song
Can cheer us; but the way seems long;
And one remembers. . . .

                                 Ah! the beat
Of weary unreturning feet,
And songs of pilgrims unreturning! . . .
The fires we left are always burning
On the old shrines of home. Our kin
Have built them temples, and therein
Pray to the Gods we know; and dwell
In little houses lovable,
Being happy (we remember how!)
And peaceful even to death. . . .

O Thou,

God of all long desirous roaming,
Our hearts are sick of fruitless homing,
And crying after lost desire.
Hearten us onward! as with fire
Consuming dreams of other bliss.
The best Thou givest, giving this
Sufficient thing – to travel still
Over the plain, beyond the hill,
Unhesitating through the shade,
Amid the silence unafraid,
Till, at some sudden turn, one sees
Against the black and muttering trees
Thine altar, wonderfully white,
Among the Forests of the Night.

1907.

Pine-Trees and the Sky: Evening

I'd watched the sorrow of the evening sky,
And smelt the sea, and earth, and the warm clover,
And heard the waves, and the seagull's mocking cry.

And in them all was only the old cry,
That song they always sing – 'The best is over!
You may remember now, and think, and sigh,
O silly lover!'
And I was tired and sick that all was over,
And because I,
For all my thinking, never could recover
One moment of the good hours that were over.
And I was sorry and sick, and wished to die.

Then from the sad west turning wearily,
I saw the pines against the white north sky,
Very beautiful, and still, and bending over
Their sharp black heads against a quiet sky.
And there was peace in them; and I
Was happy, and forgot to play the lover,
And laughed, and did no longer wish to die;
Being glad of you, O pine-trees and the sky!

Lulworth, 8th July 1907

Second Best

Here in the dark, O heart;
Alone with the enduring Earth, and Night,
And Silence, and the warm strange smell of clover;
Clear-visioned, though it break you; far apart
From the dead best, the dear and old delight;
Throw down your dreams of immortality,
O faithful, O foolish lover!
Here's peace for you, and surety; here the one
Wisdom – the truth! – 'All day the good glad sun
Showers love and labour on you, wine and song;
The greenwood laughs, the wind blows, all day long
Till night.' And night ends all things.
                                    Then shall be
No lamp relumed in heaven, no voices crying,
Or changing lights, or dreams and forms that hover!
(And, heart, for all your sighing,
That gladness and those tears are over, over. . . .)

And has the truth brought no new hope at all,
Heart, that you're weeping yet for Paradise?
Do they still whisper, the old weary cries?
''*Mid youth and song, feasting and carnival,
Through laughter, through the roses, as of old
Comes Death, on shadowy and relentless feet,
Death, unappeasable by prayer or gold;
Death is the end, the end!*'
Proud, then, clear-eyed and laughing, go to greet
Death as a friend!

Exile of immortality, strongly wise,
Strain through the dark with undesirous eyes

To what may lie beyond it. Sets your star,
O heart, for ever! Yet, behind the night,
Waits for the great unborn, somewhere afar,
Some white tremendous daybreak. And the light,
Returning, shall give back the golden hours,
Ocean a windless level, Earth a lawn
Spacious and full of sunlit dancing-places,
And laughter, and music, and, among the flowers,
The gay child-hearts of men, and the child-faces,
O heart, in the great dawn!

1908.

Day That I Have Loved

Tenderly, day that I have loved, I close your eyes,
    And smooth your quiet brow, and fold your thin dead hands.
The grey veils of the half-light deepen; colour dies.
    I bear you, a light burden, to the shrouded sands,

Where lies your waiting boat, by wreaths of the sea's making
    Mist-garlanded, with all grey weeds of the water crowned.
    There you'll be laid, past fear of sleep or hope of waking;
    And over the unmoving sea, without a sound,

Faint hands will row you outward, out beyond our sight,
    Us with stretched arms and empty eyes on the far-gleaming
And marble sand . . .
                    Beyond the shifting cold twilight,
    Further than laughter goes, or tears, further than dreaming,

There'll be no port, no dawn-lit islands! But the drear
    Waste darkening, and, at length, flame ultimate on the deep.
Oh, the last fire – and you, unkissed, unfriended there!
    Oh, the lone way's red ending, and we not there to weep!

(We found you pale and quiet, and strangely crowned with
        flowers,
    Lovely and secret as a child. You came with us,
Came happily, hand in hand with the young dancing hours,
    High on the downs at dawn!) Void now and tenebrous,

The grey sands curve before me. . . .
                    From the inland meadows,
    Fragrant of June and clover, floats the dark, and fills
The hollow sea's dead face with little creeping shadows,

And the white silence brims the hollow of the hills.

Close in the nest is folded every weary wing,
   Hushed all the joyful voices; and we, who held you dear,
Eastward we turn and homeward, alone,
     remembering . . .
   Day that I loved, day that I loved, the Night is here!

1908

Choriambics — I

Ah! not now, when desire burns, and the wind calls,
    and the suns of spring
Light-foot dance in the woods, whisper of life, woo me to
    wayfaring:
Ah! not now should you come, now when the road beckons, and
    good friends call,
Where are songs to be sung, fights to be fought, yea!
    and the best of all,
Love, on myriad lips fairer than yours, kisses you could not
    give! . . .
Dearest, why should I mourn, whimper, and whine,
    I that have yet to live?
Sorrow will I forget, tears for the best, love on the lips of you,
Now, when dawn in the blood wakes, and the sun laughs up the
    eastern blue;
I'll forget and be glad!
    Only at length, dear, when the great day ends,
When love dies with the last light, and the last song has been
    sung, and friends
All are perished, and gloom strides on the heaven:
    then, as alone I lie,
'Mid Death's gathering winds, frightened and dumb,
    sick for the past, may I
Feel you suddenly there, cool at my brow; then may I hear the
    peace
Of your voice at the last, whispering love, calling, ere all can cease
In the silence of death; then may I see dimly, and know, a space,
Bending over me, last light in the dark, once, as of old,
    your face.

December 1908

Choriambics – II

Here the flame that was ash, shrine that was void, lost in the
  haunted wood,
I have tended and loved, year upon year, I in the solitude
Waiting, quiet and glad-eyed in the dark, knowing that once a
  gleam
Glowed and went through the wood. Still I abode strong in a
  golden dream,
Unrecaptured.
          For I, I that had faith, knew that a face would glance
One day, white in the dim woods, and a voice call, and a
  radiance
Fill the grove, and the fire suddenly leap . . . and, in the heart of
  it,
End of labouring, you! Therefore I kept ready the altar, lit
The flame, burning apart.
            Face of my dreams vainly in vision white
Gleaming down to me, lo! hopeless I rise now. For about
  midnight
Whispers grew through the wood suddenly, strange cries in the
  boughs above
Grated, cries like a laugh. Silent and black then through the
  sacred grove
Great birds flew, as a dream, troubling the leaves, passing at
  length.
                I knew,
Long expected and long loved, that afar, God of the dim wood,
  you
Somewhere lay, as a child sleeping, a child suddenly reft from
  mirth.
White and wonderful yet, white in your youth, stretched upon
  foreign earth,

God, immortal and dead!
        Therefore I go; never to rest, or win
Peace, and worship of you more, and the dumb wood and the
  shrine therein.

December 1908

The Voice

Safe in the magic of my woods
   I lay, and watched the dying light.
Faint in the pale high solitudes,
   And washed with rain and veiled by night,

Silver and blue and green were showing.
   And the dark woods grew darker still;
And birds were hushed; and peace was growing;
   And quietness crept up the hill;

And no wind was blowing . . .

And I knew
That this was the hour of knowing,
And the night and the woods and you
Were one together, and I should find
Soon in the silence the hidden key
Of all that had hurt and puzzled me –
Why you were you, and the night was kind,
And the woods were part of the heart of me.

And there I waited breathlessly,
Alone; and slowly the holy three,
The three that I loved, together grew
One, in the hour of knowing,
Night, and the woods, and you –

And suddenly
There was an uproar in my woods,
The noise of a fool in mock distress,
Crashing and laughing and blindly going,

Of ignorant feet and a swishing dress,
and a Voice profaning the solitudes.

The spell was broken, the key denied me,
And at length your flat clear voice beside me
Mouthed cheerful clear flat platitudes.

You came and quacked beside me in the wood.
You said, 'The view from here is very good!'
You said, 'It's nice to be alone a bit!'
And, 'How the days are drawing out!' you said.
You said, 'The sunset's pretty, isn't it?'

By God! I wish – I wish that you were dead!

April 1909

Blue Evening

My restless blood now lies a-quiver,
   Knowing that always, exquisitely,
This April twilight on the river
   Stirs anguish in the heart of me.

For the fast world in that rare glimmer
   Puts on the witchery of a dream,
The straight grey buildings, richly dimmer,
   The fiery windows, and the stream

With willows leaning quietly over,
   The still ecstatic fading skies . . .
And all these, like a waiting lover,
   Murmur and gleam, lift lustrous eyes,

Drift close to me, and sideways bending
   Whisper delicious words.
                                   But I
Stretch terrible hands, uncomprehending,
   Shaken with love; and laugh; and cry.

My agony made the willows quiver;
   I heard the knocking of my heart
Die loudly down the windless river,
   I heard the pale skies fall apart,

And the shrill stars' unmeaning laughter,
   And my voice with the vocal trees
Weeping. And Hatred followed after,
   Shrilling madly down the breeze.

In peace from the wild heart of clamour,
  A flower in moonlight, she was there,
Was rippling down white ways of glamour
  Quietly laid on wave and air.

Her passing left no leaf a-quiver.
  Pale flowers wreathed her white, white brows.
Her feet were silence on the river;
  And 'Hush!' she said, between the boughs.

May 1909

Jealousy

When I see you, who were so wise and cool,
Gazing with silly sickness on that fool
You've given your love to, your adoring hands
Touch his so intimately that each understands,
I know, most hidden things; and when I know
Your holiest dreams yield to the stupid bow
Of his red lips, and that the empty grace
Of those strong legs and arms, that rosy face,
Has beaten your heart to such a flame of love,
That you have given him every touch and move,
Wrinkle and secret of you, all your life,
 – Oh! then I know I'm waiting, lover-wife,
For the great time when love is at a close,
And all its fruit's to watch the thickening nose
And sweaty neck and dulling face and eye,
That are yours, and you, most surely, till you die!
Day after day you'll sit with him and note
The greasier tie, the dingy wrinkling coat;
As prettiness turns to pomp, and strength to fat,
And love, love, love to habit!
                    And after that,
When all that's fine in man is at an end,
And you, that loved young life and clean, must tend
A foul sick fumbling dribbling body and old,
When his rare lips hang flabby and can't hold
Slobber, and you're enduring that worst thing,
Senility's queasy furtive love-making,
And searching those dear eyes for human meaning,
Propping the bald and helpless head, and cleaning
A scrap that life's flung by, and love's forgotten, –

Then you'll be tired; and passion dead and rotten;
And he'll be dirty, dirty!
                O lithe and free
And lightfoot, that the poor heart cries to see,
That's how I'll see your man and you! –
                        But you
– Oh, when *that* time comes, you'll be dirty too!

1909

Lust

How should I know? The enormous wheels of will
   Drove me cold-eyed on tired and sleepless feet.
Night was void arms and you a phantom still,
   And day your far light swaying down the street.
As never fool for love, I starved for you;
   My throat was dry and my eyes hot to see.
Your mouth so lying was most heaven in view,
   And your remembered smell most agony.

Love wakens love! I felt your hot wrist shiver,
   And suddenly the mad victory I planned
     Flashed real, in your burning bending head. . . .
My conqueror's blood was cool as a deep river
   In shadow; and my heart beneath your hand
     Quieter than a dead man on a bed.

1909

Town and Country

Here, where love's stuff is body, arm and side
   Are stabbing-sweet 'gainst chair and lamp and wall.
In every touch more intimate meanings hide;
   And flaming brains are the white heart of all.

Here, million pulses to one centre beat:
   Closed in by men's vast friendliness, alone,
Two can be drunk with solitude, and meet
   On the sheer point where sense with knowing's one.

Here the green-purple clanging royal night,
   And the straight lines and silent walls of town,
And roar, and glare, and dust, and myriad white
   Undying passers, pinnacle and crown

Intensest heavens between close-lying faces
   By the lamp's airless fierce ecstatic fire;
And we've found love in little hidden places,
   Under great shades, between the mist and mire.

Stay! though the woods are quiet, and you've heard
   Night creep along the hedges. Never go
Where tangled foliage shrouds the crying bird,
   And the remote winds sigh, and waters flow!

Lest – as our words fall dumb on windless noons,
   Or hearts grow hushed and solitary, beneath
Unheeding stars and unfamiliar moons,
   Or boughs bend over, close and quiet as death, –

Unconscious and unpassionate and still,
    Cloud-like we lean and stare as bright leaves stare,
And gradually along the stranger hill
    Our unwalled loves thin out on vacuous air,

And suddenly there's no meaning in our kiss,
    And your lit upward face grows, where we lie,
Lonelier and dreadfuller than sunlight is,
    And dumb and mad and eyeless like the sky.

c. 1909

Paralysis

For moveless limbs no pity I crave,
   That never were swift! Still all I prize,
Laughter and thought and friends, I have;
   No fool to heave luxurious sighs
For the woods and hills that I never knew.
The more excellent way's yet mine! And you

Flower-laden come to the clean white cell,
   And we talk as ever – am I not the same?
With our hearts we love, immutable,
   You without pity, I without shame.
We talk as of old; as of old you go
Out under the sky, and laughing, I know,

Flit through the streets, your heart all me;
   Till you gain the world beyond the town.
Then – I fade from your heart, quietly;
   And your fleet steps quicken. The strong down
Smiles you welcome there; the woods that love you
Close lovely and conquering arms above you.

O ever-moving, O lithe and free!
   Fast in my linen prison I press
On impassable bars, or emptily
   Laugh in my great loneliness.

And still in the white neat bed I strive
Most impotently against that gyve;
Being less now than a thought, even,
To you alone with your hills and heaven.

July 1909

Song

'Oh! Love,' they said, 'is King of Kings,
   And Triumph is his crown.
Earth fades in flame before his wings,
   And Sun and Moon bow down.' –
But that, I knew, would never do;
   And Heaven is all too high.
So whenever I meet a Queen, I said,
   I will not catch her eye.

'Oh! Love,' they said, and 'Love,' they said,
   'The gift of Love is this;
A crown of thorns about thy head,
   And vinegar to thy kiss!' –
But Tragedy is not for me;
   And I'm content to be gay.
So whenever I spied a Tragic Lady,
   I went another way.

And so I never feared to see
   You wander down the street,
Or come across the fields to me
   On ordinary feet.
For what they'd never told me of,
   And what I never knew,
It was that all the time, my love,
   Love would be merely you.

c. 1909

Finding

From the candles and dumb shadows,
    And the house where love had died,
I stole to the vast moonlight
    And the whispering life outside.
But I found no lips of comfort,
    No home in the moon's light
(I, little and lone and frightened
    In the unfriendly night),
And no meaning in the voices. . . .
    Far over the lands, and through
The dark, beyond the ocean,
    I willed to think of *you!*
For I knew, had you been with me
    I'd have known the words of night,
Found peace of heart, gone gladly
    In comfort of that light.

Oh! the wind with soft beguiling
    Would have stolen my thought away;
And the night, subtly smiling,
    Came by the silver way;
And the moon came down and danced to me,
    And her robe was white and flying;
And trees bent their heads to me
    Mysteriously crying;
And dead voices wept around me;
    And dead soft fingers thrilled;
And the little gods whispered . . .
                                    But ever
    Desperately I willed;
Till all grew soft and far

And silent . . .

                   And suddenly
I found you white and radiant,
   Sleeping quietly,
Far out through the tides of darkness.
   And I there in that great light
Was alone no more, nor fearful;
   For there, in the homely night,
Was no thought else that mattered,
   And nothing else was true,
But the white fire of moonlight,
   And a white dream of you.

1909

Desertion

So light we were, so right we were, so fair faith shone,
And the way was laid so certainly, that, when I'd gone,
What dumb thing looked up at you? Was it something heard,
Or a sudden cry, that meekly and without a word
You broke the faith, and strangely, weakly, slipped apart?
You gave in – you, the proud of heart, unbowed of heart!
Was this, friend, the end of all that we could do?
And have you found the best for you, the rest for you?
Did you learn so suddenly (and I not by!)
Some whispered story, that stole the glory from the sky,
And ended all the splendid dream, and made you go
So dully from the fight we know, the light we know?

O faithless! the faith remains, and I must pass
Gay down the way, and on alone. Under the grass
You wait; the breeze moves in the trees, and stirs, and calls,
And covers you with white petals, with light petals.
There it shall crumble, frail and fair, under the sun,
O little heart, your brittle heart; till day be done,
And the shadows gather, falling light, and, white with dew,
Whisper, and weep; and creep to you. Good sleep to you!

March 1910

Flight

Voices out of the shade that cried,
    And long noon in the hot calm places,
And children's play by the wayside,
    And country eyes, and quiet faces –
    All these were round my steady paces.

Those that I could have loved went by me;
    Cool gardened homes slept in the sun;
I heard the whisper of water nigh me,
    Saw hands that beckoned, shone, were gone
    In the green and gold. And I went on.

For if my echoing footfall slept,
    Soon a far whispering there'd be
Of a little lonely wind that crept
    From tree to tree, and distantly
    Followed me, followed me. . . .

But the blue vaporous end of day
    Brought peace, and pursuit baffled quite,
Where between pine-woods dipped the way.
    I turned, slipped in and out of sight.
    I trod as quiet as the night.

The pine-boles kept perpetual hush;
    And in the boughs wind never swirled.
I found a flowering lowly bush,
    And bowed, slid in, and sighed and curled,
    Hidden at rest from all the world.

Safe! I was safe, and glad, I knew!
    Yet – with cold heart and cold wet brows
I lay. And the dark fell. . . . There grew
    Meward a sound of shaken boughs;
    And ceased, above my intricate house;

And silence, silence, silence found me. . . .
    I felt the unfaltering movement creep
Among the leaves. They shed around me
    Calm clouds of scent, that I did weep;
    And stroked my face. I fell asleep.

1910

Book List

BY RUPERT BROOKE

I have not attempted to list all Brooke's published writings: this has been done admirably for all time by Geoffrey Keynes in his Bibliography (Rupert Hart-Davis, 2nd edition revised, 1954). I have omitted work which has appeared only in periodicals, and have referred all 'collected works', both verse and prose, to the most accessible sources.

Letters from America, Charles Scribner, New York, 1916; Sidgwick & Jackson, 1916

John Webster and the Elizabethan Drama, John Lane, New York, 1916; Sidgwick & Jackson, 1916

Lithuania: a Drama in One Act, Stewart Kidd, Cincinnati, n.d.; Sidgwick & Jackson, 1935

The Death of John Rump in Edward Marsh, *A Number of People*, Heinemann, 1939

The Poetical Works, ed. Geoffrey Keynes, Faber & Faber, 1946

Democracy and the Arts, Rupert Hart-Davis, 1947

The Prose (selected), ed. Christopher Hassall, Sidgwick & Jackson, 1956

The Letters (selected), ed. Geoffrey Keynes, Faber & Faber, 1968; Harcourt Brace Jovanovich, New York, 1968

'A or B?' (paper to the Apostles) and other hitherto unpublished pieces in Timothy Rogers, *Rupert Brooke: a Reappraisal and Selection*, Routledge & Kegan Paul, 1971

ABOUT RUPERT BROOKE

This is a mere selection of books (biographical and critical) which have Brooke as their main subject, or in which he makes a significant appearance.

Asquith, Herbert, *Moments of Memory*, 1937

Bayley, John, *The Romantic Survival*, 1957

Bonham Carter, Lady Violet, *Winston Churchill as I Knew Him*, 1965

Browne, Maurice, *Recollections of Rupert Brooke*, 1927

Bullough, Geoffrey, *The Trend of Modern Poetry*, 1934

Clements, Keith, *Henry Lamb: the Artist and His Friends*, 1985

Dalton, Hugh, *Call Back Yesterday*, 1953

de la Mare, Walter, 'Rupert Brooke and the Intellectual Imagination' (first published in a limited edition, 1919, and later revised and included in *Pleasures and Speculations*, 1940)

Garnett, David, *The Golden Echo*, 1953, and *Flowers of the Forest*, 1956

Grant, Joy, *Harold Monro and the Poetry Book Shop*, 1967

Hassall, Christopher, *Edward Marsh: a Biography*, 1959, and *Rupert Brooke*, 1964

Hastings, Michael, *The Handsomest Young Man in England*, 1967

Holroyd, Michael, *Lytton Strachey* (vol. 1), 1967

Johnston, John H., *English Poetry of the First World War*, 1964

Lehmann, John, *Rupert Brooke: His Life and His Legend*, 1980

Levy, Paul, *G.E. Moore and the Cambridge Apostles*, 1979

MacKenzie, Norman and Jeanne, *The First Fabians*, 1979

Marsh, Edward, *Rupert Brooke: a Memoir*, 1918, and *A Number of People*, 1939

Nesbitt, Cathleen, *A Little Love and Good Company*, 1974

Press, John, *A Map of English Verse*, 1969

Rogers, Timothy, *Georgian Poetry 1911–1922* ('The Critical Heritage'), 1977

Ross, Robert H., *The Georgian Revolt 1910–1922*, 1967

Sassoon, Siegfried, *The Weald of Youth*, 1942

Stead, C. K., *The New Poetic*, 1964

T[ownshend], E., ed. *Keeling Letters and Recollections*, 1918

Wilson, Colin, *Poetry and Mysticism*, 1970

Woolf, Leonard, *Beginning Again*, 1964

Woolf, Virginia, ed. Mary Lyon, *Books and Portraits*, 1977 (see also her *Letters*, vol. 2, 1976, and *The Diary*, vol. 1, 1977)

Index of Titles

Index of First Lines

201

The Long March
William Styron

'HAS A GRANDEUR THAT COMES FROM BEING
PERFECTLY DIRECT, YET DEEPLY IMAGINATIVE ABOUT A
VERY SIMPLE THEME, CHOICELY ELOQUENT AT THE
NUMBERLESS LEVELS THAT MARK ALL THE GREATEST
WRITING'
SUNDAY TIMES

THE LONG MARCH

Lieutenant Culver had been called off the Korean War reserve list
to take part in manoeuvres in South Carolina. Colonel
Templeton, a regular Marine, disgusted by the soft condition of
the men, ordered them to take part in a thirty-six mile forced
march – to get them into combat shape . . .

It was a severe and unnecessary exercise, fraught with tension and
misery as Culver watched his sensitive Jewish friend and
co-Reservist, Captain Mannix, pit his will against Templeton's in
an abortive attempt to express his frustrated sense of injustice –
and to reveal the crass stupidity of the whole military system . . .

0 552 99300 X

BLACK SWAN

Cobweb Walking
Sara Banerji

'A book which exercises a compelling fascination and reveals an original and highly imaginative mind at work'
THE LONDON STANDARD

As a child – so tiny and delicate that her father calls her fairy – Morgan has a special relationship with nature, for she can hear the Silence – the humming of the Silence is her secret, even from her beloved father, as is the day that she walks along a cobweb.

But with adolescence comes a loss of childhood innocence and the intrusion into her perfect world of an unwanted stepmother and baby sister. Her privileged position in the household is usurped. She begins to learn the uncomfortable truth about her strangely sheltered existence, and slowly her thoughts turn to revenge.

'The inner depths of this creature are explored with skill. The change from hate to love is a hard chemistry to analyse but Banerji succeeds'
SUNDAY TIMES

0 552 99220 8

BLACK SWAN

Ellen
Ita Daly

'A startling first novel. Initially the charm, sharp observation and slight self-mockery are reminiscent of a Jane Austen heroine. By the end Ellen has become something far more sinister'
JULIAN ALEXANDER, LITERARY REVIEW

An only child of Catholic Dublin parents, Ellen was a strange, solitary girl. She was lumpish and dull, she was lonely. But she had resigned herself to this, and wanted nothing more from life than to be left alone in her isolation, to carry out a quiet typing job without interference, without change. If only her mother would stop entertaining such ambitious fantasies for her. When Ellen's hopes of an academic career fell through, Mrs Yates moved on to visions of a glittering social success, inviting strange girls around for elaborate teas and friendships which never materialized.

Then Ellen met Myra. Pretty, rosy Myra who wanted Ellen to be her friend, to meet her family, to share a flat! A new world unfolded, a world which Ellen found completely voluptuous; evenings by the fire, fish and chip suppers, secrets shared with a friend – even if that friend could sometimes be casually brutal. Throughout the summer months, there were lazy days spent in the garden with Adrien, Myra's stockbroker boyfriend and his cousin. Bobbie even paid attention to Ellen. She had never imagined that life could be like this, and she wanted it to go on forever. Who would have thought that the idyll could be violated – let alone in the shocking way it was?

'A first novel that is formidably subtle and fluent'
GILLIAN SOMERVILLE-LARGE, THE IRISH TIMES

'An intriguing and disturbing picture of a moth in the glare of a flashlight'
COSMOPOLITAN

'ELLEN is a deftly promising first novel'
CHRISTOPHER WORDSWORTH, THE GUARDIAN

0 552 99251 8

BLACK SWAN

As We Forgive
Barbara Neil

'Obsessive love, loneliness, despair, guilt and incest are all deftly brought into this ambitious work, which would be a praiseworthy achievement even for a seasoned writer; as a first novel it is an extraordinary accomplishment.'
PUBLISHERS WEEKLY

The happiest moments of Lydia's childhood had been those spent at the home of her wealthy friend Nathalie. Nathalie, with her rosebud nightgowns, her governess, and her magnificent father, Ben Wavell, was everything that Lydia longed to be – and never could be.

When the adult Lydia met Ben Wavell again she found him a sad, middle-aged man deserted by both wife and daughter but still, for Lydia, he shone as the glamorous figure of her childhood, still exerting the sexual pull that she was now old enough to recognise. Once more her life was to be dominated by the Wavells as she was sucked into an obsessive and sexually overwhelming situation.

'This first novel is heady and forbidden fruit. In immaculate and at times inspired prose, the taboo act of incest is gradually revealed.'
BOOKLIST

'She has taken on two difficult problems, a delicate theme and some aggressively articulate characters. The theme she handles with exquisite control, establishing an almost psychic relationship with her readers.'
NEW REPUBLIC

0 552 99260 7

BLACK SWAN

Final Payments
Mary Gordon

'Genuinely distinguished . . . a first novel of extraordinary quality'
LOS ANGELES TIMES

Now Isabel Moore's father is dead she must – at 30 – finally face the world. She has been safe until now from its temptations, from its promises of passion and pleasure, from the urgings of her own body, from all the sweet whisperings of life. No longer safe, Isabel discovers that she is beautiful, that men desire her. More disturbing still, she discovers that she desires them. Almost overnight she has turned from a 'good Catholic girl' into a warm, vital woman, hungry for life – hungry but also very confused, and very frightened.

'One of the best novels of any kind I have read in recent years . . . tremendously enjoyable, a little like Mary McCarthy, a little like Margaret Drabble, yet really, like nothing but itself. Read it'
SUSAN HILL, THE TIMES

'Impressive and entertaining'
NEWSWEEK

'Original, perceptive, highly intelligent and remarkably honest'
MARGARET DRABBLE

'Versatile, original . . . defies summary and stereotype. Read it'
HARPER'S MAGAZINE

'Electric prose'
NEW YORK TIMES

0 552 99212 7

BLACK SWAN

The Killeen
Mary Leland

'Sheer good writing in the traditional narrative manner'
THE GUARDIAN

A killeen is a small graveyard, often situated at a crossroads. It
was customary to bury the bodies of unbaptised babies there and
the little cemeteries can still be found throughout the Irish
countryside.

In Mary Leland's novel, set in Cork in the 1930s, the killeen can
be seen as Ireland itself, in its early years as an independent state,
an emergent nation still inhospitable to individual aspirations.
And it is against the harsh background of the new republic that
the overlapping story of three young people is played out.

'Mary Leland in this book has opened a dozen doors for the
imagination; her shadowy people in their vivid landscape will
haunt as ghostly figures always do. It is a story of people who
love, but it is in no way a love story. Those who love most lose
most, and that is possible the most haunting memory of all in
this finely crafted book'.
MAEVE BINCHY, IRISH TIMES

'Her grasp of the vulnerability and inner strength of human
beings is noteworthy.'
SUSAN HILL, GOOD HOUSEKEEPING

0 552 99203 8

BLACK SWAN